INSIDE THE CONCENTRATION CAMPS

Eyewitness Accounts of Life in Hitler's Death Camps

Compiled by
Eugène Aroneanu

Translated by
Thomas Whissen

PRAEGER

Westport, Connecticut
London

Library of Congress Cataloging-in-Publication Data

Konzentrationslager. English
    Inside the concentration camps : eyewitness accounts of life in
Hitler's death camps / compiled by Eugène Aroneanu ; translated by
Thomas Whissen.
        p. cm.
    Includes bibliographical references and index.
    ISBN 0–275–95446–3 (alk. paper).—ISBN 0–275–95447–1 (pb : alk.
paper)
    1. World War, 1939–1945—Concentration camps. 2. Holocaust,
Jewish (1939–1945)—Personal narratives. 3. World War, 1939–1945—
Atrocities. I. Aroneanu, Eugène. II. Title.
    D805.A2K6613 1996
    940.53'18—dc20   96–120

British Library Cataloguing in Publication Data is available.

Library of Congress Catalog Card Number: 96–120
ISBN: 0–275–95446–3
        0–275–95447–1 (pbk.)

First published in 1996

Praeger Publishers, 88 Post Road West, Westport, CT 06881
An imprint of Greenwood Publishing Group, Inc.

Printed in the United States of America

The paper used in this book complies with the
Permanent Paper Standard issued by the National
Information Standards Organization (Z39.48–1984).

10 9 8 7 6 5 4 3 2 1

This book is dedicated

to the memory of

Walter B. Birk

Colonel in the Polish Army

Loving husband of

Teréz Birk Brecher

Devoted father of daughters

Carolyn and Angela

Survivor of four and a half years in

Dachau and Auschwitz

Deceased 1968

"All that is necessary for the triumph of evil
is for good men to do nothing."

Edmund Burke

"Sometimes, there is only
one side to a story."

Edward R. Murrow

"Ere their story die."

Thomas Hardy

Contents

Preface

These eyewitness accounts of life and death in the Nazi concentration camps of the Third Reich are shocking, touching, moving, and unforgettable. They are stories of unbelievable horror, unbearable suffering, and incredible courage. Millions perished under circumstances of unimaginable degradation, their voices silenced, seemingly forever. Fortunately, the war ended before the Nazis could finish their hellish job, and thousands of prisoners survived to tell us their own stories as well as the stories of those whose lives had been so cruelly and so casually terminated.

These accounts chronicle, in grisly detail, unspeakable crimes against helpless, innocent people. What is important to remember is that they are true stories told by people who were there and saw with their own eyes the atrocities that were committed hourly against anybody the Nazis did not like. If you were too old, too young, too fat, too thin, you could be disposed of. They would work you until you dropped, then kill you for the crime of exhaustion. They enjoyed punishing one person for another person's "crimes" or slaughtering hundreds of hostages on the slightest pretext. Ultimately, in an act of diabolical irony, they could kill you simply because you had seen too much and could testify to what you saw. After all, the last thing they wanted to leave behind was an eyewitness.

Fortunately, many eyewitnesses did survive. And fortunately Eugène Aroneanu was passionate enough about Nazi crimes against humanity to conduct interviews and record the accounts of 100 of these survivors who had been interned in camps throughout Germany and German-occupied territory.

In translating these accounts, I have taken care to preserve the tone and style of the speakers. These are not literary people making literary statements. They are people from all walks of life who try to express the reality of the nightmare they survived as sincerely and straightforwardly as they can. They seldom exaggerate. If anything, they are modest in their statements, often reluctant or unable to render monstrous deeds in graphic terms, preferring instead to rely on euphemisms, or to fall back on commonplace adjectives like awful, terrible, and horrible. But sometimes the very banality of their expressions has greater impact than the phrase that strains for effect. These statements sound genuine; they have the ring of truth.

Any editing I have done has been limited to emendations for the sake of clarity, consistency, and continuity. I have also pruned the occasional redundancy, but I have not otherwise tampered with the contents. Thus, if some entries seem contradictory, it is because each section is made up of the statements of prisoners from many different camps. Under the circumstances, what is impressive is not the trivial differences in their accounts but their overwhelming similarities.

I chose to translate this book for several reasons. First, I hoped to achieve a level of empathy with the victims and maybe even somehow penetrate the twisted minds of their oppressors. In both endeavors I can only say I think I came as close as anybody can who wasn't there. Second, although I certainly wanted to remember and honor the victims who died in the camps, I also wanted very much to honor those who survived, for it was by their survival that Hitler's "final solution" was defeated. Their eyes have become the windows through which we can glimpse the ordeal all prisoners endured. Third, I found in these accounts overwhelming evidence that the torture and carnage was widespread and indiscriminate. These eyewitness accounts tell of heinous crimes committed against a great array of "undesirables": Catholics, Communists, Czechs, Danes, Dutch, English, French, Greeks, Gypsies, homosexuals, Hungarians, Jehovah's Witnesses, Jews, Norwegians, Poles, Russians; the list goes on. No one was safe. Anyone could end up in a death camp. That's one of the harrowing lessons of this book.

I am indebted to Teréz Birk Brecher, the brave Hungarian lady who first brought this book to my attention. I am also indebted to my wife, Anni, for lending me her keen translator's ear.

Above all, I want to express my gratitude to Eugène Aroneanu, a man so deeply disturbed by the enormity of "crimes against humanity" that he gave his life in the struggle to expose and eradicate this evil. May this translation of his book help keep his spirit alive.

Thomas Whissen, 1996

Introduction

"The bigger the lie," said Hitler, "the more easily people fall for it." About this Hitler didn't lie, for his big lie was believed.

Today this lie has borne fruit. To the millions of soldiers who died in the war that Hitler started can be added the greater number of victims the Nazis murdered in cold blood in the concentration camps. Ten million is the lowest official figure; twenty million would be closer to the truth.

The greater the crime, the harder it is to believe. This tendency toward self-deception can be found in all who took Hitler's teachings to heart. Even now they act as if they doubt the crimes the Nazis committed, preferring rather to ignore them. In so doing, they implicate themselves in the crimes. There is an old French proverb that says: "One only goes in the direction one is inclined."

If noble-minded Germans want to build a new Germany, how can they know how this Germany should be created if they have no idea what to replace the old with? How will the Germans of tomorrow be able to fulfill their duties properly if the Germans of today ignore the legacy of yesterday's Germany, namely the crimes of the Third Reich?

Naturally it is fitting that the criminals be punished. But it would be better yet if no crime had been committed, as much for the sake of society as for the would-be criminals. Justice can call a temporary halt to it, but only those who work against it can remove the causes. Of course, to remove them, they first have to recognize them.

In the following work, however, we do not concern ourselves with the moral or legal character of crimes against humanity. This is a totally factual report of shameful deeds which, if it fulfills its purpose, will convince the reader that it is not right to persecute or murder people because of their religious or political views or because of their race or nationality.

Those who have not renounced the Nazi ethos will learn nothing from reading this work, for it contains nothing that can surprise or injure them. They would be ready at any time to begin again, and the only observation they would make is the same one that can be read in the testimonies of any one of the Nuremberg defendants: "They should have got rid of all of them while they were at it!"

A French humorist once said: "The idea that people in the hereafter are happy is nonsense since nobody ever returns from the hereafter." Well, some did return from the Nazi hereafter. What troubles the Nazis the most is not the monstrous crimes they committed but the fact that eyewitnesses lived to tell about them.

So it is that we turn in brotherly love to all well-intentioned Germans, to those who have experienced the tragedy of Germany and remained uncorrupted, to those who are willing to cooperate in the creation of a government worthy of the best of the German tradition.

Traditionally, we have been inclined to think of crimes against humanity as crimes against common law. It would follow, then, that the world would have no reason to be alarmed since every nation has its penal code. If that were so, then Nazi Germany, which also had its penal code, would not have committed all these crimes. And if that were the case, then such a limited number of hangmen could never have executed such an enormous number of victims. If that were really so, then the German public authority would have been sufficient to end these shameful deeds without first requiring the invasion of the Allies.

Crimes against humanity are only vaguely related to crimes against common law. As long as society is subordinate to common law, the victim always retains the possibility of seeking help from public authority. In the case of crimes against humanity, those concerned stand there completely powerless. No one interferes, not the police, not the mayor, not anybody. Public authorities are no longer able to provide protection to those who innocently come in conflict with the penal code.

And that's not the only thing. Because public authorities don't see to it that common law is respected, they become accomplices in the crimes against humanity through their participation in the arrest of the victims.

But it goes even farther than that. The railroad transports the victims, civil servants execute the laws, the press stirs up hatred in the people, manufacturers build gas chambers and ovens, doctors exceed their authority, the pharmaceutical companies test their medications on prisoners, the financing of the whole nefarious business is assured, and the authorities, all authorities, keep quiet without exception, just as long as they are not held accountable for the smooth running of the operation.

"It is an organized, state-supported bloodbath that takes place in broad daylight under the very eyes of a horrified humanity," said Professor Trainine.

Orders were given only once, and they were carried out, not, as one might think, because they should be, but because they could be. From the German lawmakers, civil servants, and high government officials down to the ordinary hangmen, to the government, the army, the party, the SS, the Gestapo—all the machinery of the Third Reich—everyone was ready and willing. The iniquitous civil system did exactly what was required of it.

By means of ordinances and various public or secret decrees, this civil system resulted in National Socialist legislation that deprived four categories of people—who had in no way violated the criminal law— of their rights and declared them guilty of something that would be futile, not to mention degrading, to deny: namely, the fact that they were members of a particular race or citizens of a particular country or held a particular religious or political view. As a result, it was not possible either to defend or punish people according to the normal penal code, and this exception was used to the disadvantage of certain classes of people. This bypassing of the penal code was perpetrated by the same authority that is supposed to guarantee its validity: by the state, which is the ultimate expression of national sovereignty.

So, for reasons of race, religion, politics, or nationality, human beings were deprived of the protection society had forged over the course of centuries: the penal code.

Committing a murder is without a doubt a violation of the penal code. To ignore this code and deny to an entire group the protection that every civilized society grants the innocent is a violation of the basic principles on which a society rests. It is just as Judge Jackson expressed it at the Nuremberg trials: "The real plaintiff at this bar of justice is civilization."

The same authority that circumvented the penal code to the disadvantage of certain categories of victims went even one step further when it actually sanctioned the perpetrating of crimes. The executioners were officially recognized by the state, and their power was unlimited. The Nazi state put at the disposal of its executioners the means by which their authority could be increased a hundred- or a thousand-fold, depending on how efficiently they could execute victims. The primary violator of the common law was the Nazi state itself in its moral, judicial, spiritual, and material embodiment of all those who contributed in one way or another to the formation of this state and carried out its orders.

The collective character of the criminal finds a counterpart in the collective character of the victim. This collective character derives not from the fact that the victims were murdered "collectively," but that they were accused collectively. They were condemned only because of what they were, not for anything they had done.

The determining "intent" in the case of crimes against humanity is totally different from that in the case of crimes against common law because in the first case the victim is judged not as an individual but only as a member of one of the pertinent categories: race, nationality, politics, religion. When the victim can prove that he does not belong to any of these categories, then he avoids his fate and the hangman doesn't carry out the execution. He ignores his "individual" victim and considers him only as belonging to the group of victims who are being considered. The blood that touches the hand of the hangman is impersonal blood; it is the blood of an abstract "person," not that of a certain individual. The hangman only fulfills an unpleasant duty conscientiously. One cannot talk to him about guilt in this case. The ultimate responsibility rests on those who have imposed this duty on him and who have made a regular target out of the collective "person."

The real source of the evil lies in the Nazi teachings, the agenda of the Nazi party, in everything, in fact, that led to the formation of the Nazi state. At this moment, when the accused in Nuremberg use as their defense the democratic methods by which Hitler had come to power as well as the voluntary concurrence of so many German voters for the Nazi program, at this moment when Germany would again enjoy its democratic freedom, it is essential to focus one's attention on conscientious Germans, and in particular on the seriousness of the election, because it was this kind of election back then that was the reason Germany embarked on the road to inhumanity. It is just as necessary, however, to point to the spirit that the whole civilized world wishes would rule in Germany in future years.

In compiling these eyewitness accounts of crimes against humanity, we have proceeded exactly the way an examining judge would proceed. The statements of 100 sworn witnesses and 25 official reports form the basis of this report. We have used only those sources that provide new information and contribute to the understanding of the whole. The number cited at the end of each entry identifies either the witness testifying or the report from which the statement was taken. This document, then, represents the experiences of hundreds of victims whose individual stories corroborate each other, especially in details and particulars. Thus, by means of these many witnesses, the individual speaks, and the voice of the "human person" is heard.

We have chosen not to interfere by making any commentaries or interpretations. We have let the victims tell their own experiences with complete freedom.

Since the treatment of women as workers deviated considerably from that of men, we have devoted a separate section to that in chapter 6. In all other cases, we have proceeded without differentiating between the two so that sometimes the narrative moves from the male to the female experience without grammatical distinctions.

We believe, then, that we have clearly and distinctly documented the crimes against humanity that were committed by one and the same state wherever this state had any power, throughout its existence, in wartime as well as in peace time, against the same victims.

Eugène Aroneanu, 1946

A Note About
Eugène Aroneanu

Born in Rumania, Eugène Aroneanu emigrated to Paris in the mid-thirties, a young man with a law degree and a passion for justice. After war broke out in September 1939, he directed radio broadcasts to Rumania. When France was occupied in 1940, he joined the resistance, operating underground under the name of Arène. In 1943 he escaped to Switzerland.

Aroneanu devoted his life to exposing and combating "crimes against humanity." He was the author of 58 publications—books, articles, legal studies—all leading to one major treatise: "International Penal Law in the Light of the Present World." In 1945 he was given the task of drawing up the first tables of Nazi atrocities for use at the Nuremberg trials. The result was this book, a compilation of eyewitness accounts, hailed at the time as a "haunting work" and "the naked and definitive truth." He was the first to classify testimonies, the first to reveal the inner workings of the camps, the first to list the names and functions of over 400 locations in which millions died; the first to publish terrifying photographs of unparalleled horror.

When Eichmann was arrested in Argentina and brought to Israel, there were scholars who contested the arrest. Aroneanu's response was insistence on international law. "To find the way back to the law," he said, "one must first find the way to justice." His life was totally committed to justice and protecting human rights through international law. He died prematurely in 1960.

List of Witnesses, Reports, and Documents

1. Adler, Julien Ochs
2. Amar Cathérine (attorney)
3. Arditi, Pierre
4. Azoulay, Maurice
5. Bachmann (grade school teacher)
6. Bader, Jean (merchant)
7. Balachowski, Dr. Alfred (Pasteur Institute)
8. Barbier, Henri (professor)
9. Bich-Mochet
10. Bloch, Claude (biologist)
11. Bortuso, Louis (bakery clerk)
12. Cartier-Worms, Henriette (lawyer)
13. Champy, Christian (professor of medicine)
14. Chavassine, Madeleine (engineer, chemist)
15. Chemel, Pierre (student)
16. Clément, Maurice (merchant)
17. Cliquet, Charles (physician)
18. Cohen, Maurice (radio technician)
19. Coudert, Charles (physician)
20. DeGombert
21. Durand, Albert
22. Errera, Samy
23. Feigelson, Raphael
24. Fradin, Georgette (physician)
25. Freismuth, Joseph
26. Fresnel (physician)
27. Gaßmann, Marcel

28. Gelis (journalist)
29. Geneste, René (army officer)
30. Girard, François (student)
31. Girard, Louis-Lucien (physician)
32. Goldet (nurse)
33. Goldlist
34. Goldstein, Felix
35. Goldstein, Henri (physician)
36. Greil, Léon, Dr. (physician)
37. Grimaud, Pol Emile (prefect)
38. Gritz, Richard
39. Gueroult
40. Henoque (abbot)
41. Hereil, Jacqueline (social worker)
42. Hodebert
43. Kohn, Alex
44. Kuziner, Paul
45. Lajeunesse
46. Lauth (professor)
47. Laval, Edouart-José (mayor, orthopedic surgeon)
48. Lebegue, Andrée (sales clerk)
49. Le Bellon de Dione, Jacques (army officer)
50. Lecuron, F.
51. Le Du
52. Le Gigan, Jean (sales manager)
53. Legrand, Suzanne (social worker)
54. Leloir, Dr. (professor of religious history)
55. Leon-Kindberg, Michel (physician)
56. Lepadier, Mina
57. Lequeu
58. Magescas, Armand
59. Manhes, Henri-Frédéric (colonel)
60. Marbler
61. Marquet, Yvonne
62. Martin-Chauffier, Jean (medical student)
63. Martin-Chauffier, Louis (writer)
64. Mazeaud, Léon (professor of law)
65. Monestier, A.
66. Morey, Bernard (manufacturer)
67. Morlais, Anne-Marie (social worker and court assistant)
68. Naparstek, Charles (dental technician)
69. Nègre, Maurice (journalist)
70. Paul, Marcel (electrician)
71. Paul, Sylvie

Numbers preceding the names of the above witnesses, reports, and documents correspond to the numbers at the end of the entries in the document that follows.

Incomplete identification of some witnesses reflects oversights in the original documentation due almost certainly to the difficult circumstances under which these testimonies were gathered and processed.

Chapter 1

The Nazis' Four Main Reasons for Internment

RACE

"On the 4th of May, 1943, I was arrested in a police raid at the Marseille train station at the very moment I presented my identity card stamped 'Jew.'" (87)

NATIONALITY

"Two shipments of Czech civilians arrived at the camp in March 1942 and were taken immediately to the mobile gas chambers and then cremated in the ditches." (86)

RELIGION

"I was not apprehended for taking part in any particular activity but simply for being chaplain of the underground forces; in other words, for performing my priestly duties. They told me that I was guilty of the offense of abusing my office and would be sentenced to death." (54)

POLITICS

"Because I was a member of the Communist party, there was a warrant out for my arrest as early as September, 1940." (71)

Chapter 2

Deportation

DEPARTURE

"The trainload of prisoners carried between 1,000 and 1,200 persons—men, women, children, old people—of all classes and nationalities." (93)

"Among them were mothers carrying newborn babies, frail old people on stretchers, seriously wounded people, small children. An SS guard, who had been dispatched by car to an orphanage to bring back the children, returned without them saying that he just couldn't bring himself to do it. So the company commander sent another bus to get the children, and this one, after several trips, eventually brought back 350 orphans for deportation. Although the children were given thermos bottles, condensed milk, and bottled water at the beginning of the trip, most of them died along the way." (6)

"The SS stripped us completely naked and squeezed 140 persons into one boxcar. These were the famous WWI boxcars they said could hold 40 men or 8 horses. It was sheer hell." (51)

"The boxcars were thoroughly sealed." (20)

"We couldn't sit, we couldn't even crouch." (7)

"What I ended up doing was spending the night on one leg, since there wasn't enough room to stand on both." (69)

"In the middle of the car was a bucket that served as a chamber pot; in a few hours it was full to overflowing and gave off a terrible odor. After that, people had no choice but to relieve themselves directly on the floor, and that meant that we spent the trip enveloped in a poisonous stench.

"During the trip there were numerous attempts to escape. . . . These attempts were extremely dangerous and were not possible in most cars. We couldn't try anything because our car was next to that of the SS and was constantly under surveillance. The main escape attempt took place during the second night while we were still in France. Someone managed to get a door open while someone else broke a window and pried loose the iron bars. When the SS discovered the attempt, the train was stopped and the hunt began, with help from search lights on nearby towers and from machine guns located at each end of the train. The SS poured forth from their cars in pursuit of the escapees and fired at them.

"The last car of the train, which had remained empty, was reserved for corpses. It contained not only the dead but also the wounded who were thrown in together with the dead. I saw this car again at Buchenwald and heard the moaning and groaning of the wounded. I know with absolute certainty that all of them were killed and thrown in the ovens along with those already dead." (7)

"These attempts to escape were cruelly suppressed." (50)

"In the cars from which the escape attempts took place, the prisoners were stripped naked and a great many of them were shot like criminals on the spot." (78)

"I witnessed executions being performed in a bomb crater just outside the boxcar." (30)

"A few young people were hastily selected. . . . We saw five of them approaching from among the first to be chosen; each was accompanied by a German policeman carrying a handgun. The moment they reached the ditch, a policeman would grab hold of a prisoner, stand him against the wall, and shoot him in the head." (69)

"Before they moved on, the comrades of those just killed would cover the bodies with a few shovelfuls of earth." (30)

"The trip took 8 to 10 days, during which we were given soup and bread only twice." (55)

"It took 10 days and 9 nights to complete the trip from Cherbourg to Hazebrouck (near the Belgian border)." (4)

"All of us were racked with thirst. I saw some of my comrades pushed to the point of drinking their own urine, others to licking the sweat off the backs of fellow prisoners, while still others tried to catch the occasional drops of water that condensed on the walls of the boxcar." (54)

"At the terminal in Bremen we were denied water by the German Red Cross, who told us that there was no water for us." (29)

"We were half dead from thirst. In Breslau we begged the nurses of the German Red Cross for water, but they remained deaf to our pleas. No water, stifling heat, no air (the vents were blocked)." (10)

"At every stop you could hear voices from the boxcars begging for air. Without fail a German officer would reply: 'You have everything you deserve.' At every station those who managed to open a window and beg the guards for help got either a bullet from a revolver or a burst from a machine gun for an answer." (92)

"Two comrades died of suffocation. I myself was busy until dawn taking care of my friend P. who had heart trouble." (69)

"By five o'clock we counted about 100 who had suffocated; after that the number mounted rapidly from minute to minute." (92)

"From every car there were reports of outbreaks of madness. Some of the prisoners had no choice but to silence others who had become either crazed or dangerous." (78)

"In one car there were horrifying cases of mass insanity in which the prisoners killed each other with excessive brutality." (92)

"I saw with my own eyes a shipment of prisoners who had all gone totally mad." (69)

"In one shipment 64 deportees arrived dead. They had all died of suffocation." (54)

"In my boxcar there were 82 dead out of 126 alive at departure. I have no doubt that similar conditions existed in other boxcars." (51)

"By the time we got to the camp, we counted 896 dead." (92)

"Of 1,200 French deportees, only 500 arrived alive." (51)

"My shipment, which started out with 2,500 prisoners, lost 912 along the way because of conditions that ranged from unspeakable to unbearable." (37)

ARRIVAL

"We arrived in the middle of a pitch black night. Visions of horror. Visions of terror. The most tormented hours of my imprisonment. Cries of wild animals, unholy howling. What was it all about? The reception by the jailers, accompanied by their huge, well-trained wolfhounds. We were so afraid our legs buckled. We knew we would never leave this place." (120)

"The boxcars were forced open and the SS guards stormed in. Shouting wildly, they prodded us with rifle butts and bayonets and beat us with clubs, then set the dogs loose on us. Those who fell and could not get up were ripped apart. I was wearing a large cape which the dogs sank their teeth into, forcing me to submit." (7)

"We had to unload the boxcars not just of the suitcases but also of the dead and the dying. The dead—and that included anybody who could not stand up—were tossed onto a pile. The suitcases and packages were gathered up and the boxcars were scrubbed down so that no trace remained of their hideous contents." (104)

"Right there by the train the SS killed most of the children. M. W. saw both of his little boys collapse at his side." (123)

"The French were shot down on the arrival platform by the SS." (71)

"I saw one SS guard grab a child by the feet and throw it into the air while a cohort fired his pistol at this living target. Another SS guard yanked a baby from its mother's arms and tore it apart by putting his foot on one leg and pulling on the other." (23)

"An officer strode forward and announced an inspection. Everybody was ordered to undress, and then he asked for an accounting of the 'refuse.' By 'refuse' he meant the dead. There were 954." (20)

"One shipment included 800 corpses out of 2,500 deportees. To begin with, the deportees had had to cover nearly 80 kilometers on foot. Then they had been put into open trucks in which they traveled for eight days." (30)

"The most gruesome spectacle I witnessed was the arrival of shipment after shipment of prisoners, especially the one that came from Großkoyn. There were 3,000 prisoners at the outset, and they had been made to travel 60 kilometers on foot without a break, all the while deprived of food, and constantly beaten. Then they were loaded onto open trucks, 100 to a vehicle, and forced to crouch down in a huddle. The first to stand up got shot. They traveled this way for seven days and seven nights. They arrived with 700 dead and 700 so sick they died soon thereafter. The rest climbed down out of the train, and those who couldn't make it to the camp were shot." (31)

"The largest shipments of French deportees arrived at the camps in June and July of 1944. It was then I saw corpses I will never forget. The Nazi monsters had squeezed 100 to 140 people into each boxcar. I remember in my own case, where there were only 50 to a car, that we still could neither breathe nor move, and I wondered how people could survive under these circumstances. The people I now saw arriving had all died of asphyxiation. Their faces had turned black, and their lips were horribly swollen. There were several truckloads of corpses in this condition. To perform any burial rites was, of course, out of the question; these bodies had to be hauled to the ovens without delay. Sadly, they still had their civilian clothes on and were carrying photographs of their families with them. That was in July 1944, and the ovens were working night and day." (90)

"They separated the women, the children, and the old people from the rest of the deportees, and that was the last we ever heard of them. I think that my wife, who was among them, went with them to the gas chamber." (55)

"The prisoners filed past an SS guard who pointed out the direction they were to take: to the left, men between 20 and 45 and young women—in short, those who could work; to the right, the rest of the prisoners, older women, children, the elderly, the sick, the 'unusable' —the 'wasteful mouths.'" (20)

"As we were led from the railway station to the camp, we were beaten with clubs and menaced by dogs." (71)

"In spite of our weakness we had to travel the five kilometers from the station to the camp on foot." (50)

"The SS guards had stolen our shoes back at the border, the moment we were across, so we had to hike barefoot through the snow and the filth." (123)

"With hammer blows to our backs and sharp kicks in the shins, these animals ordered us to march swiftly but silently. No lagging, no infirmity was tolerated. My comrades, already fatigued from the weight of their suitcases, lived in mortal fear of these twin gangs: the SS and their dogs." (120)

"Most of the prisoners were not capable of going on. All those who couldn't keep up were left by the roadside, and we never saw them again. I can testify to this with absolute certainty because I worked in the hospital. Everything points to the fact that they were killed." (79)

"The distance had to be covered running; the old who could not run fell behind and were finished off with clubs." (7)

"A few days later 700 Russians arrived in the same condition as their predecessors. They were famished and looked like wild animals. They were guarded by German soldiers who would shoot at the slightest provocation." (125)

"A shipment of Jews from Budapest, who had traveled the whole way on foot through the snow, arrived at the camp. Since they had had nothing to eat or drink for a week, they had eaten snow. Upon their arrival, they were ordered not to sit down, and we other prisoners were told to move closer to them. From time to time one of them would keel over dead. Behind this convoy came the dump trucks on which several hundred frozen bodies were piled. Unloading them was like unloading iron posts." (19)

"Thousands of these poor creatures, driven forward by the SS men and their dogs, died from exhaustion or were shot down like animals in the street and left to die in the snow." (71)

"Before we entered the camp, there was an examination of the prisoners who had been added to our shipment. Each prisoner was summoned and had to give his name. If he pronounced his name in French and the Germans couldn't understand it, he received a blow with a rubber truncheon. Once, an SS guard about 17 from Transylvania beat the new arrivals unmercifully on the back with two rubber truncheons." (86)

"In the doorways and hallways, eager young SS guards were positioned to strike the new arrivals with their fists or rifle butts or kick them with their boots. In a sort of anteroom there were 20 prisoners with their faces pressed motionless against the wall. With curses and blows the new arrivals (French, Russian, Polish, Belgian, German, etc.) were made to understand that they would be treated like these poor 20 if they turned their heads or as much as moved a finger. But regardless of how obedient they were, most of them were beaten anyway without having any idea why. From time to time someone would call out, 'Next.' Since most of prisoners didn't understand German, nobody moved. Those who were supposed to step forth would then be viciously beaten. Many fell down and were kicked. The torture continued inside the office. . . . I was more dead than alive when it came my turn to go inside." (27)

"Two huge guards beat the arriving prisoners with leather thongs." (58)

"For my part, I got three teeth knocked out and a split lip, courtesy of an SS officer. They hit us the from the moment we arrived at the camp." (75)

"As the number of overseers increased, the abuse increased along with it. They competed to see who could hit the hardest and punch the most savagely." (120)

"It was almost dark. We had to march in rows of three and in lock step to cover the 100 yards to our barracks. We were surrounded by SS guards. Anyone who did not march in step or got a little out of line or turned his head was either kicked or struck with the barrel of a gun. When we got to our barracks, we were ordered to go to cell 4. Then, accompanied by punishing blows, they pointed out our cells, none of which had a number." (27)

"Young girls were whipped. They received 30 lashes on their backsides. This was carried out in the presence of the camp Kommandant, a doctor, and the chief overseer." (120)

Chapter 3

Internment

RECEPTION

"The moment we set foot inside the camp we were given a tattoo on the left forearm." (20)

"I was branded with a red-hot iron." (89)

"We were no longer a personality; we were just a number." (120)

"The children, even the infants, were tattooed. When the Russians liberated the camp, they found a two-week-old baby with a number tattooed on its arm." (86)

"To be 'disinfected,' we had to take all our clothes off. Our ears and other body parts were inspected to see if we were hiding anything. Then we moved to another room where all our hair was shaved off with electric razors and shearing machines." (7)

"No hairy part of the body escaped the razor." (54)

"We looked on helplessly as women lost their hair to the shearing machine." (120)

"In general, 7 out of 10 women were shorn; we had no idea how that number was established." (41)

"Of the 964 women in our group, approximately 600 were shorn. It seemed to be done arbitrarily, without a system." (28)

"As they sheared us, they gave us soothing assurances: 'Animal fabrics are warmer than vegetable fabrics. Therefore, calm yourselves, nothing is wasted, German industry utilizes everything. With your hair we'll make blankets, clothing for the SS, etc.' Actually, while we had nothing to put on, the dogs of the SS wore coats (with the SS monogram) that often had been made from our hair." (72)

"Next we were herded into a shower room where we were immersed in a huge tub filled with a phenol solution. The very sick died as they were lifted from the tub because the procedure was very agonizing. Others lost consciousness and could no longer stand up." (7)

"I saw one old Frenchman whose comrades had lifted him from the boxcar and escorted him through the disrobing to the shearing and then finally to the shower room. There two Nazi thugs beat him up. Then one grabbed him by the shoulder, the other by the feet, and they tossed him into the tub where he died. Then they threw him in a corner." (62)

"Brutally they shoved us [women] into a room adjacent to the showers. There, five at a time, we were 'thoroughly' searched. I emphasize 'thoroughly' because even our vaginas were carefully inspected. The SS matrons took turns conducting this inspection, moving from one prisoner to the other, without ever washing their hands, and with no regard for the young girls, all this in the presence of the SS guards and their dogs, which lunged at the naked prisoners if they so much as stirred." (120)

"The Germans made up a chart for each of us and entered nonexistent illnesses on it. I, for example, was listed as having lung and heart problems when even today, after so much suffering (typhus, double pneumonia, etc.), the examination I recently underwent revealed that my lungs are completely sound, while the weakness in my heart is a result of the treatment I received during four and a half years imprisonment, two of them in Germany itself. The Germans arranged it so that any death could appear to be the result of natural causes." (72)

"They took our civilian clothes and all of our personal possessions. Nothing was to remind us of our homes." (120)

"Then we were given rags to wear (which gave them an opportunity to steal our clothes) and a pair of wooden sandals with only a simple strap over the toes to hold them on with. This forced the wearers to lift their feet high with every step.

"The camp was particularly overcrowded at those times when new shipments of prisoners arrived. There was literally no room to receive the new arrivals. Sometimes the prisoners had to wait two or three days before space could be found in the barracks. During this time they remained out-of-doors without food because they didn't officially belong to the camp as long as they had not yet been assigned to a barracks. The result of such waiting was that many prisoners came down with pneumonia, bronchitis, etc." (54)

"We slept for ten days on wet earth, without blankets, without straw, and naturally without fire. In November 1939, after the war in Poland, somewhere around 2,000 Polish prisoners of war arrived at the camp. Under the pretext of delousing they had to undress in the freezing cold and were then crowded together in a cramped barbed-wire enclosure; their clothes were burnt. For food they received a tenth of a loaf of bread per day. At the end of three weeks only ten of them were left. All the rest had died of cold and hunger." (106)

THIEVERY

"Dutch and French Jews said the Germans had told them they were leaving their homelands in order to be taken to Poland where they could continue to work at their professions, and that they would be compensated for every business, every enterprise, every factory confiscated by the Germans. They were to take along their prize possessions and enough cash to last them at least six weeks. Consequently, a considerable amount of money and valuables ended up in the camp." (104)

"They took our money from us and all our jewelry." (125)

"The SS and the Gestapo oversaw all operations." (20)

"While these various operations were in progress, I saw the guards brazenly stuffing their pockets with valuables and money.

"Driven by avarice and greed, leading personalities in the party, both junior and senior officers, repeatedly filled their pockets with jewelry, gems, bearer bonds, and foreign currency.

"I could not bring myself to hand over my wedding ring, so, right after I was captured, I swallowed it. I did this two more times." (57)

"Along the way a young SS guard, about 20, approached me and said to me in French: 'Give me your wedding ring.' I didn't answer. He hit me hard, and then for the next five kilometers he kept prodding me on the back and shoulders with the barrel of his gun. After five kilometers I passed out. With his feet he rolled me into a ditch, and as I came to, he tried to remove the ring with the blade of his knife. He finally succeeded in removing it after he had spit on my finger in order to get the ring off. With more blows he forced me to my feet and pushed me into the back row." (88)

"The exact number of gold teeth each prisoner possessed was carefully recorded in a register." (65)

"They pulled out the teeth of the prisoners in their search for diamonds, claiming that they could easily be concealed in a hollow tooth. They also extracted crowns, but they didn't record these extractions in the register." (110)

"They used tongs to pull out all my gold teeth." (89)

"The Germans urged us to write to our families and include a printed notice advertising the existence of a canteen and stating that we were allowed to receive money orders so that we could buy things in this canteen. Naturally the canteen did not exist." (58)

"They never gave me back the money they had taken out of my billfold; nor did they give me the money my wife sent me—25 marks a month for 4 months. I discovered upon my return to Paris that the Gestapo, who had arrested me in my apartment on August 15, 1942, had also taken the sum of 225,000 francs in banknotes from my desk along with 180,000 francs in treasury bills." (31)

"For special jobs the camp tormentors used prisoners, usually volunteers, like, for example, a certain young Luxemburger whose specialty was searching for jewelry in the vaginas of dead women." (55)

"The name 'Canada' was given to a camp organization which employed 1,200 men and 2,000 women. There, materials of all kinds taken from the trainloads of prisoners were sorted, packed, and shipped to Germany: clothing, food, medications, toilet articles, jewelry, pictures, underclothes, tobacco, cigarettes, bedding, and human hair. Within this organization the Germans had trained a group of specialists to scrounge among the clothes and bedding for gems and other valuables that the owners might have overlooked." (31)

"All the stuff stolen from the prisoners was carefully organized and shipped to Germany. In the gigantic shoe warehouse in Camp #6 there were shoes with labels from Paris, Vienna, Brussels, Warsaw, Trieste, Prague, Riga, Antwerp, Amsterdam, Kiev, Krakow, Lublin, Lvov, and other cities; shoes of every size and style, for men, women, young people, small children, combat boots, ordinary boots, farm boots. In addition, the warehouse also contained a huge number of shoemaking materials (soles, insoles, heels), that had been selected, sorted into piles, and made ready for shipment to Germany.

"In this death camp alone there were hundreds of thousands of shoes that had once belonged to men, women, and children who had been tortured and killed.

"In the big Gestapo camp on Chopin Street in Lublin there were huge quantities of men's, women's and children's underclothes as well as all sorts of personal belongings. For example, there were drawers full of balls of yarn, thousands of eyeglasses, tens of thousands of men's, women's, and children's shoes, tens of thousands of neckties with labels from various cities: Paris, Prague, Vienna, Berlin, Amsterdam, Brussels—thousands of women's corsets; a portion of these had been sorted out and made ready for shipment. Robes, pajamas, slippers, toys, milk bottles, shaving sticks, scissors, knives, and a large variety of household items. Among the spoils there was also a mountain of suitcases that had once been the property of citizens of Russia, Poland, France, Czechoslovakia, Belgium, Holland, Greece, Croatia, Italy, Norway, and Denmark.

"SS Colonel Ternes declared, in his capacity as former camp finance director: 'As for me, I know that the money and valuables taken from the prisoners were sent to Berlin. The gold taken from the prisoners was shipped according to weight. All these stolen valuables amassed significant revenue for the German Reich. Considerable quantities of gold and valuables were sent to Berlin. I know all this firsthand because I worked in the camp as director of finance. I know for a fact that large quantities of gold and valuables were not listed on the incoming invoice because they had been stolen by the Germans who confiscated them.'" (111)

CLOTHING

"The clothing was totally inadequate. From time to time we were inspected, and any clothes we had other than the prescribed official 'uniform' were taken away. Some prisoners might trade two or three days' food rations for a sweater only to have it confiscated, along with anything else that wasn't permitted, including even the paper clothing many prisoners wrapped themselves in to protect themselves from the cold. Personal garments were removed from the old, the sick, and the crippled. Coats were forbidden; jackets and shirts alone were allowed." (73)

"We were paralyzed with cold in the morning, for even at this time of year, we were not allowed to wear a garment made of wool." (120)

"In rainstorms we were completely soaked and our coarse wool clothes weighed us down to the point where we could no longer wear them. They added several kilos which the women were unable to sustain. We were forced to stop and wring them out all day long because we had no fire to dry them by." (67)

"The wooden shoes we had been issued caused inflammation that, because it went unattended, often resulted in death." (86)

HOUSING

"50 wooden barracks and 20 concrete buildings for 16,000 people—that was the reality of a concentration camp." (69)

"All of these buildings were constructed according to a master plan. Each unit was approximately 100 feet long and 25 to 30 feet wide. Although the walls were scarcely six feet high, the roof rose another 15 feet to a height, at its peak, of 22 feet. The room was divided into two parts by a partition. Along the outside walls and the walls of the partition were three levels of narrow cells. Normally three persons lived in each cell. These cells were so narrow there was scarcely enough room to lie down, let alone sit up or stand up. In this way between 400 and 500 persons were 'accommodated,' as they put it." (104)

"There were 750 of us in one barracks that was 150 feet long and 30 feet wide, with 12-foot-high walls halfway up the sides, sloping to a 20-foot-high peak at the top of the ceiling. By April 4, 1945, the number of prisoners reached 1,350. Inside, however, there was room for only 936 persons to lie down, which meant that you were lucky to sleep two nights out of three. Those who couldn't lie down remained sitting on benches or standing. In some barracks the overcrowding was even worse, and I was told that on many nights as many as 2,100 persons were crammed into a single barracks." (80)

"It was virtually impossible to breathe in this air." (7)

"When we arrived, the sleeping accommodations appeared to be quite nice; the beds had been neatly made, and on each straw mattress there was a small, blue-white coverlet that was almost pretty. But unfortunately our contentment did not last long. When we turned down the corner of the coverlet, we saw that the mattresses and covers were crawling with vermin. My blanket was filthy." (28)

"We slept on mattresses that were filled with sawdust." (60)

"There were 10, 11, even 12 of us in a cell 12 feet long, 6 feet long, and about 5 feet high. The head of every prisoner pressed against the feet of his neighbor." (80)

"There was not enough room to sleep on one's back." (7)

"During the night, whenever you wanted to turn, you had to poke your comrades so that you could all turn at the same time. We lay like sardines, crosswise and flattened on our sides." (59)

"The women no longer menstruated. Of ten suffering women you could be sure that nine had dry ovaries, because the Nazis would not let them sleep stretched out. There were between 1,200 and 1,300 of them." (57)

"The women slept in the latrines and even out-of-doors, sometimes at temperatures as low as 20 degrees below zero." (9)

"The camp could accommodate between 25,000 and 40,000 people. There were times when the number of prisoners was as high as 45,000. The number of internees in this camp was not exceptional.

"The prisoners of war in the camp included members of the former Polish army, who had first been taken captive in 1939, plus prisoners from Russia, Poland, France, Belgium, Italy, Czechoslovakia, Greece, Yugoslavia, Denmark, Norway, and other countries." (111)

FOOD

"Nutrition was at a lower than subsistence level." (80)

"Not enough to stay alive on and too much to die from." (23)

"At 7 in the morning 'coffee' was distributed: dirty water that came from melted snow; that was it." (125)

"The meals were anything but good: nettle leaves, cabbage, and beet roots, a few potatoes, a piece of bread with something that vaguely resembled marmalade or an ersatz cream cheese; that was it." (50)

"The bread consisted of 40 percent potato flour, 25 percent chestnut flour, 20 to 25 percent barley flour, and the rest was sawdust." (29)

"Bread rations were unpredictable; they fluctuated between 150 and 250 grams. That was very disconcerting for us since we never knew how much we would get to eat. The food was disgusting." (61)

"Even in the soup there were rotten vegetables that caused frequent outbreaks of dysentery." (14)

"Frequently the soup served to the internees was mixed with a chemical that caused dysentery and hemorrhaging. All medications were ineffective." (38)

"Dinner was often cold because it had been brought to the barracks at four o'clock while roll call might last until six o'clock or later." (60)

"The soup would stand outside so long it would turn into a block of ice. Only then was it distributed." (38)

"We were not allowed to have knives, and at one point they also took away our spoons. We were forced to slurp our soup." (12)

"One prisoner had a plate, another a gas mask canister, another a rusty tin can. Everybody ate out of makeshift utensils." (125)

"Every parcel sent to us was confiscated and we were given only the empty boxes." (11)

"During the four months I spent there, we received nothing from the Red Cross." (76)

"No package ever got into the hands of the prisoners." (83)

"I saw packages arriving from the French Red Cross marked 'For the Steward of the French Internees.' The SS guards explained to us that these so-called 'stewards' did not exist and, therefore, they could dispose of the packages as they wished, which is what they did." (98)

"All of our packages were regularly stolen. We saw the head matron eating some things from France and we knew where they came from. In the garbage bins we found the empty sardine cans and the wrappings from the little rectangular cookies made back home." (28)

"Before our very eyes the women officers sold the civilian factory workers packages of food that had been confiscated from our rations." (12)

"Theoretically the prisoners received the above-stated rations, but in reality most of them were stolen before they ever could be distributed." (104)

"Furthermore, a considerable amount of coffee, soup, or breakfast got wasted because we had to eat on the double while trying to avoid the guards who stood along the way and kept us moving with blows from their clubs and their boots. This wasn't too hard for the young people who were athletic enough to avoid these obstacles along the way, but there were old people and crippled people to whom the same regulations applied. The raw brutality of this barbarian horde was unleashed on these hapless victims." (27)

"In order to get our meals, we had to stand in line while blows from clubs rained down on our heads. They ladled out this 'boiled water' in such large amounts that we could not carry our bowls without spilling their contents; and we were not allowed to slow down but had to keep running, which meant more blows to our ribs and almost nothing left in our bowls." (74)

"The soup and the 'coffee' were distributed in 50-liter vats. These vats, which were a lot like those used by the French army, weighed 60 pounds empty and 100 pounds full, not counting the lid.

"Seven pots were required for the morning or evening brew; fourteen for the soup. These pots were hard to handle; two or four persons could carry them but only with difficulty because you had to be careful not to burn yourself since the pots had no lids. The poor women who had to lug these pots tried hard to walk in step in order to keep the sloshing to a minimum and not burn themselves, but it was very hard, all the more so because the way back was quite far (the farthermost barracks being a good mile from the kitchen) and the street was dirty and slippery and full of holes, so that in many places they sank to their knees in filth. It was sheer torture. If they slowed their step, the SS guards would use their clubs to prod them forward. Used to suffering, most of them pushed themselves to the limit, but their physical condition could not match their attempt to be brave. Many would faint, either from fatigue or because of the beatings. Then the pots would overturn and the soup would spill out, which was just what the Germans wanted. Since the contents were not replaced, all the prisoners suffered because all of them had to take the blame, and so each individual ration was reduced. This incident was repeated frequently. Thus the already insufficient rations, which were constantly being reduced anyway, were reduced even more." (57)

"It was extremely difficult to receive even a spoonful of soup. Of the many prisoners who tried, only a fraction succeeded. The others were kicked and beaten." (12)

"To get any food, we had to stand outside in the rain and cold, sometimes for an hour and a half, for the distribution." (28)

"To get any soup, we had to obey the officers who ordered us to line up 500 feet from the distribution point and then crawl the whole distance. When we got there, they ordered us to run back to the line and then hop all the way forward again while they kept beating us. If we were lucky enough to get any soup, we didn't know where we were supposed to go eat it. Some of us just stood in the hallways, others went into the latrines." (12)

"The first time I went to get my soup, I had to crawl on my hands and knees even though my physical condition was extremely weak." (88)

"During the distribution of food the following scenes occurred daily:

If the line got too close to the distributor, the head guard would 'distribute' blows, usually with a large cane or club without watching where he was hitting. If the line got too far away from the distributor, a similar scene was enacted for the opposite reason. If, for example, a new arrival happened to stick his head out of the line a little to see what he was supposed to do to get his ration, that, too, was a reason to be beaten. Usually the ever vigilant overseer would grab the offender by the hair and pound his head against the barracks wall, kick him, and send him away without food." (27)

"As a result of overcrowding, the already inadequate food rations came to a halt and we got only soup once a day." (53)

"It was often the case that for days on end the internees would be given nothing to eat or would receive only a fraction of the rations that were rightfully coming to them." (106)

"The children were constantly tormented by hunger. No sooner was the distribution over than we had but one desire: food. We were not allowed to eat during roll call. If it is hard enough for a grown up to resist the temptation to eat when he is hungry and holding a piece of bread in his hand, then it has to be torture for a child. An SS woman kept a sharp lookout, and every three or four days she would catch some poor kids eating. Immediately the culprits would be dragged before the group, their food would be taken away for the whole day, and they would be punished in the following way: They had to kneel down in a line with their faces to the sun, a large rock on their heads, their arms raised, and in each hand a brick or cobblestone. They had to remain in this position until the end of roll call, sometimes two or three hours, or until they were exhausted." (57)

"We couldn't sleep because we were so hungry." (103)

"Starving, we scrounged around in the garbage for cabbage roots which, for us, were a real find. To illustrate what lengths we were driven to by our hunger: One day we women were sent out to plow under a field of rape seed; instead, we ate the plants. After we finished, you would have thought a swarm of grasshoppers had stripped the field clean." (28)

"The inmates ate grass, just as it grew." (67)

"We were so weak when we were finally freed from this hell that many of us still died from hunger and exhaustion." (40)

"The American doctors attested to the fact that the bodies of the adults weighed only 60 to 80 pounds. In most cases they had lost 50 to 60 percent of their normal weight and even their size." (106)

"Whenever an autopsy was performed, there was atrophy of the heart muscles, shrinking and yellowing of the liver, and an absence of mucous membranes in the stomach and intestines.

"The intestines of the prisoners suffering chronic diarrhea—known also as 'flux'—were the thickness of cigarette paper. In contrast to what went on in other camps, the dysentery bacillus had not taken hold here; therefore, it followed, that the camp 'flux' was the result of a lack of food high in protein (egg whites, eggs, red meat, etc.)." (86)

"The effects of this diet were scientifically monitored. Each new arrival was weighed in order to ascertain the average weight of all the prisoners. After a certain period of time, they were weighed again in order to gauge the extent of their emaciation. Then a regular report, written according to specific regulations, would be sent to the authorities comparing the average weight loss of the new prisoners to the average weight loss of the rest of the camp." (65)

"The meager rations given to the prisoners caused them to die from malnutrition. We found out that in a camp nearby, people were often disposed of in this way." (31)

"Prisoners were regularly starved to death; numerous cases of exhaustion and death occurred because of debilitation. They fed on offal, they ate cats and dogs. Most of the internees were nothing but walking skeletons, mere skin and bones, or else they were grossly fat because of the swelling brought on by hunger.

"Mr. M., a professor at the Collège de France, was literally starved to death. I saw how he tried to join a group that was washing dishes just so he could try to get some food by scraping the edge of the bowls with his fingers." (47)

"One Frenchman, who had once lived near the 'Place de la République,' a former member of the Foreign Legion, father of two children, a wounded veteran with many scars on his body, died of hunger." (98)

"Incidents of cannibalism were not unheard of." (90)

"The misery of the prisoners was so great that many of the corpses were chopped into pieces and the pieces cooked and eaten. I saw that with my own eyes. I also saw bodies that were missing a chunk of thigh, or a heart, or even testicles (a particular favorite)." (63)

HYGIENE

"No showers, very little water." (125)

"Since we slept in our clothes, we had to undress with lightning speed if we wanted to wash up because once that door opened, God help those who did not appear naked immediately in front of the spigot. And God help those who after half a minute had not run back inside their cells. If an internee got only three lashes in this time period, he could consider himself lucky. Under these conditions it was not possible to wash more than your face." (38)

"The water was dirty; in general there was only one spigot for up to 10,000 women. To get water you had to stand in the snow or a puddle of water." (14)

"1,400 people had to wash in a room big enough for at most 60 persons, and all the washing had to be done in an hour, which was simply impossible. As a consequence, most prisoners didn't even try to wash. One overseer stationed at the door speeded up the washing with a rubber truncheon." (86)

"At the baths two German prisoners convicted of multiple thefts and murders began beating up on us as we jumped into the tank. Some of my comrades were quick enough to escape with only a few blows. Others, however, were unable to reach the edge of the tank before their brains were already oozing out of their skulls." (101)

"It was the middle of August, and we didn't have any drinking water. We were given water only for washing dishes, but we used it for drinking anyway—and at those times when the women absolutely had to have it for reasons of personal hygiene. We would give them a quarter liter of water that we had pilfered." (42)

"For feminine hygiene there was, of course, no warm water, no soap, no sanitary napkins, only dirty rags." (125)

"One day the German matrons who guarded us noticed that in the afternoon we still had some water left and that we were holding back a bit of soup for the children's supper. They immediately took it all away from us." (24)

"The women helped each other bring water from the far end of the camp. On a bitter cold evening, they would carry buckets of water to wash themselves with. Dead tired from work, stuck in a wretched camp, cooped up in filthy barracks without light, without heat, forced to sleep on straw, like dogs." (125)

"Most of the prisoners got only polluted water in the latrine; they came down with dysentery, and many of them died from typhus." (63)

"The toilet consisted of 12 wooden buckets set up at the entrance to the barracks. To think that these could serve the needs of 700 people was absolutely ridiculous. The overflow from these improvised toilets ran down the length of the barracks and onto the planks on which the prisoners slept." (83)

"In Birkenau the toilet was on boards above a ditch." (43)

"In the field the toilets were out in the open." (60)

"Awful things occurred in the latrines. Sometimes a woman would have a miscarriage, then wrap the newborn in paper and throw it in the ditch." (125)

"Right after breakfast all the inmates would be assembled and led in a group to the latrine. Permission to do this was granted only once a day. Women who were caught urinating in the vicinity of the barracks were punished with 10 to 25 blows depending on their physical condition. Often we saw how these poor creatures would be beaten so badly for this offense by the SS matrons that a few hours later they would be dead." (57)

"If dysentery forced you to get up at night, it was usually impossible to make it to the latrine in time. Naturally, the camp was covered with excrement, and when a woman could no longer reach the latrine and was surprised by a guard or an overseer, that meant a terrible beating." (10)

"The barracks were full of fleas." (7)

"The overflow forced us to lie four or five to a straw mattress, and it was impossible under these conditions to get rid of the vermin. It was also impossible to wash in a room 12 feet long and nine feet wide with 12 spigots for 500 people when we were given only half an hour.

"I hadn't changed clothes for four months, and my clothes were finally falling off me in rags. Since we killed between 100 and 200 lice per day, their juices stained our clothes red, brown, and black and caused them to stiffen when dry. One time a prisoner, who had not been able to wash his shirt, took it off and let it stand by itself." (88)

"Because of this total lack of hygiene, we became prey to all manner of vermin. The nights, which were short enough as it was, were interrupted by the bites of fleas and bedbugs; body lice and head lice were our constant daily companions. There were so many of them that we couldn't shake them off." (37)

"If a woman finally succeeded in ridding herself of lice, she would turn around only to face the same nuisance from the vermin-infested blankets. One night I was given a blanket and within an hour I was infested with thousands of lice." (67)

"One day they decided to delouse us. All the women and children had to undress completely. They smeared a pomade on all the hairy parts of our bodies and then everyone in the barracks was crowded together and made to sleep on the bare floor. In the night the dogs were let loose and countless women and children were bitten. Whoever wanted to escape the bites had to climb up on the wardrobes. After two days and a night spent like this, we had to endure a roll call during which we were forced to stand naked for two hours in a snowstorm before we could return to the barracks. When we finally got back to the barracks, we found that the covers of the straw mattresses, along with the blankets, had been taken away, and we had to sleep on putrid straw and sawdust in which lice existed in sickening profusion." (72)

"In order to be allowed a few hours sleep you had to completely disrobe, in spite of the weather, and be deloused. Those who lacked the strength or were too worn out to care were soon covered with suppurating wounds. A few of my comrades didn't undress for months." (83)

"Eventually, you learn to suffer all kinds of torment: open sores, skin rashes, unbearable pain, etc." (120)

"Many women had skin rashes and dirty black blisters. Others had large pimples. Most had sores on their feet from the constant marching and the continuous work; they were crawling with vermin, their hair was chopped off, and they were forever scratching themselves. The Germans did not touch them, nor did they come any nearer than five yards when they wanted to speak to them. . . ." (125)

"Fleas, bedbugs, and lice were everywhere—spreading typhus." (60)

Chapter 4

Administration and Camp Regulations

ADMINISTRATION

"The Camp Commander, a brutal SS lieutenant, was the scourge of the camp.

"The Supervisory Personnel consisted of SS men from the 'Death's Head' Division. The officers were Germans, while a large number of the troops were made up of Poles, Rumanians, Hungarians, and Croatians. There were also volunteers." (60)

"The Inner Administration of the camp was handled by specially selected prisoners. People were not billeted by nationality but by profession. Each Block was run by a team of five people consisting of the senior prisoner [the person who had been in the camp the longest], a Block secretary, a medic, and two assistants.

"The Senior Prisoner wore an armband with the number of his Block, and he was responsible for maintaining order in that Block. He decided between life and death. Before February 1944, nearly half of these elders were Jews, but a directive from Berlin put an end to this situation. All of them had to relinquish their offices except for three Jews who were permitted to keep their posts in spite of the directive.

"The Block Secretary was the senior prisoner's right-hand man. He ran the office and busied himself with file cards and registration. His work carried a lot of responsibility with it, and he had to keep his books with painstaking precision." (104)

"Barracks Bosses and 'Kapos' [from Italian 'capo' for 'chief'] were common German criminals who had been in camps or prisons for 8, 10, 12 years . . . and who, encouraged by the Nazis, launched a reign of terror over us." (60)

"The barracks bosses proved to be invaluable accomplices in the Nazi extermination scheme. They had the power of life or death over all of us." (57)

"In addition to a pack of 200 German wolfhounds, which were an important part of camp security, there was also a contingent of 'Battle Police' called 'Rescue Police,' made up of common criminals." (111)

"Prisoners were divided into work squads; at the head of the squad was a German convict, or Kapo. The most visible symbol of his office was his club. All the Kapos were professional criminals." (60)

"The barracks orderlies got their positions on the basis of certain connections which also gave them certain prerogatives. They mistreated us as badly as the SS. Among them were all nationalities including Russians, Ukrainians, and Poles. The Red Army soldiers might have made good orderlies, but they were too intractable, so all the foreign barracks orderlies were chosen instead from among the rabble." (59)

"Two-thirds of the barracks bosses, the Kapos, and the foremen were murderers, con men, and forgers who could decide whether we lived or died, and they routinely abused this power with impunity." (63)

"There was no possibility of resistance against these Kapos because the least attempt meant death, which the SS not only tolerated but sanctioned. For example, a young Russian who had dared to protest was beaten to death with a whip by a Kapo. After being questioned by the SS, the Kapo was heartily congratulated for the vigorous way he maintained discipline." (7)

"The women lived in circumstances similar to the men, the only difference being that they were guarded by SS matrons." (110)

"We women were under both a female and a male commander who were assisted by a large number of SS matrons. We called them 'lady officers.' We rarely came in contact with the leader of the camp." (2)

"The 'lady officers' were mostly convicted criminals. The one who was in charge of our Block had been sentenced to life in prison for killing both her parents.

"A lot of young prison matrons learned how to handle female prisoners by practicing on us. These trainees were, for the most part, ordinary German girls. However, there were also many women from occupied countries such as Rumania, Holland, Greece, and Czechoslovakia. These women had been forcibly recruited." (53)

"One time the German authorities were short of SS matrons, so they recruited them by force from the factories without even giving them enough time to inform their families. They were taken to the camp where they were divided into groups of 50. One day they were put to the test. An internee, chosen at random, was brought before them and they were told—all 50 of them—to hit her. I remember that out of all of them, only three women asked the reason why, and only one woman refused to do it, which caused her to be thrown into prison herself. All the others quickly got into the swing of things as if they had been warming up all their lives for it." (72)

"Each block of 300 to 400 deported women was under the command of a 'Blockova' or 'Stubova,' who had the power of life and death over the other inmates. I myself saw and heard one of them say to a poor girl who had managed to acquire a pair of beautiful boots: 'Give me your boots or I will personally shove you into the oven.' Which she did, without hesitation, when the girl refused.

"In general, that was the mentality of the 'Block Chief' or 'Blockova.' They lacked for nothing: jewelry, furs, clothes, money, food. It is not surprising that many internees, for their own protection, contrived, or to use a German expression, 'put themselves in a position,' to do whatever it took to supply their block leader or 'Blockova' with whatever she wished." (57)

"This demoralization of the people, this indiscriminate chaos that degrades when it does not destroy, this chaos where criminals and patriots are intimately bound together, had been deliberately planned by the Nazis." (69)

"In *Mein Kampf* Hitler had formulated the idea that prisoners guarding other prisoners was an excellent way to pit the victims against each other—to foment hatred and disgust, to encourage denunciations, in short, to debase a person. And those who put this idea into practice contributed their own refinements. They drew on the violent nature of the common criminal. The convict became the jailer." (53)

"No camp rule was ever posted or in any way announced to the prisoners." (27)

"No camp rules existed. Nothing specific was forbidden, undoubtedly because everything was forbidden. An action permitted one day would result the next day in prolonged ill treatment by the SS." (45)

"It was the law of the jungle and justice was arbitrary." (69)

"Because the registration cards contained only the numbers, not the names, of the prisoners, errors were unavoidable. Say, for example, that the secretary happened to record a death sentence incorrectly. Because of the exorbitant number of deaths, the mistake would simply result in the death of the bearer of the wrong number. Corrections were not allowed. The Block secretary had a privileged position that made frequent abuse possible." (104)

"The SS did not interfere in personal disputes." (17)

"A 'green' prisoner could kill a 'red' one. A person was found dead one day who had been drowned in a tub and then tossed into the street where he was run over by a machine and crushed. So they pitched him into an oven while the SS looked the other way. No investigation, no commentary; life goes on." (69)

"The only explanation the SS gave to the prisoners was that no prisoners living in this place would ever be allowed to leave." (50)

"The SS personnel who ran the camp felt secure in the knowledge that all the inmates, whether prisoners of war or internees or whatever, and of whatever nationality—Russians, Ukrainian, Polish, White Russian, Jews, French, Greeks, etc.—would sooner or later be killed and that no one who knew what happened would ever live to tell it. This certainty applied especially to those who controlled the behavior of the guards and who decided on which methods of extermination were to be employed. The dead are mute and can tell nothing. And details can be neither imparted nor confirmed through documents alone. Therefore, no one would ever have tangible proof, and that was what mattered most to the Germans." (110)

"In May 1941, a staff officer of the SS killed H., a Jewish man. This caused the witnesses to this murder (30 in all) to be killed because H.'s brother, who was one of the witnesses to the murder, complained about the arbitrariness of the act, giving details about the participants, including their names." (105)

DIFFERENCES BETWEEN PRISONERS

"The internees in the camp came from all levels of society and were divided into the following categories:

—real criminals
—political prisoners
—homosexuals
—so-called 'work avoiders' [goldbrickers]
—military personnel of all ranks who were guilty of a serious disciplinary violation, especially insubordination.

This last category was called the 'SAW,' i.e., Sonder-Abteilung Wehrmacht [Special Section of the Wehrmacht]." (96)

"Each prisoner wore a registration number on the left breast and right thigh. Directly under the number was a triangle of colored cloth. Stamped on the triangle was the nationality of the prisoner: F for French, P for Polish, R or SU for Russian, etc. The German prisoners wore nothing to indicate their nationality." (60)

"The meaning of the colored triangles was as follows:

Red triangle: political prisoners under supervision
Green triangle: common criminals
Black triangle: relapsed criminals
Pink triangle: homosexuals
Purple triangle: Jehovah's Witnesses

The Jewish prisoners were differentiated from the Aryan prisoners in that the red triangle could be transformed into a Star of David by the use of yellow thread." (101)

"NN - *Nacht und Nebel* (Night and Fog) meant: sentenced to death. This name, *Nacht und Nebel,* was taken from a secret organization of the Dutch resistance movement." (17)

"In the camp nobody knew exactly just what NN stood for except that, as far as we could tell, certain people were never assigned to the details that worked outside the camp." (122)

"Among the deported women were some who belonged to category NN. Among them were Marie-Claude Vaillant-Couturier and Geneviève de Gaulle, both of whom had been forced to submit to very harsh treatment." (114)

"All the prisoners were treated equally, without regard for status or nationality." (104)

"We women had become half vagabonds and half bagnio slaves: all differences had disappeared. The designation 'political internee' was the biggest joke that ever was. When I got here as a political prisoner in a shipment of exclusively political prisoners, they dressed us in striped prison clothes and made us realize that this was simply a prison, to which were added the 'joys' of physical punishment (like 25 lashes or solitary confinement) and nothing to eat." (122)

Crudely carved on a fence post of a camp is the ironic slogan of Germany's national anthem. The date is 1912

Factories of death grimly await the arrival of hordes of unsuspecting victims

Primitive bunks into which sick and dying prisoners were squeezed. Those underneath suffered most

Desolation, exhaustion, despair

A prisoner tries to carry a mug of "boiled water" back to the barracks without spilling it

Goaded by guards, prisoners would often fall and lose their rations

Chapter 5

Life in the Camps

DISCIPLINE

"The one word that best describes camp life is 'monotony.' Everywhere we turned, we came up against the so-called Kapos (relapsed German criminals) who were armed with rubber truncheons." (101)

"Blows to the head and beatings were daily occurrences that no one looked upon as anything out of the ordinary." (122)

"Even the sick were kicked and beaten." (59)

"The treatment was the same for all, the French as well as the Germans and other nationalities." (17)

"Orders were given only in German. Those of us who did not understand German and could not immediately respond to the orders were kicked, slapped, and so on." (44)

"In a 10- to 14-day period, I received a total of 175 canings on the buttocks. During this same time, I was forced to hang by my wrists once a day for 25 minutes." (38)

"Often you would see maybe 30 prisoners who had been beaten with rubber hoses and who had sustained anywhere from 50 to 70 bruises." (82)

"One SS guard would use anything he could lay his hands on—a rubber truncheon, a shovel, whatever—to beat any prisoners who came near him, for no reason whatsoever. When columns were formed, he would amuse himself by behaving like a madman, kicking and beating those unfortunate enough to be in his way. We called him 'the Cudgel' because he always carried a club with him with which he randomly attacked the prisoners." (4)

"Another SS guard took a particular pleasure in herding the prisoners out of their cells and making them kneel until their heads touched the ground. Then he would stomp on their heads with his iron-heeled boots until blood gushed from their noses and ears." (38)

"One unit leader was totally crazy. He ranted and raved for no reason at all. He'd make the prisoners stand at attention before him and then give them a kick in the stomach." (30)

"He'd throw men in the mud, then let them crawl out, only to throw them in again. He did it to add variety to the routine blows to the head, the genitals, the stomach, etc." (39)

"Even age didn't count, except as a sign of weakness, something that only invited beatings. Because he had the audacity to sit down on his straw pallet, General B. de F., who was 80, was beaten unconscious.

"When the camp commander detected any violation of camp discipline, he would torture us with senseless and malicious punishments which he called 'sport.' For up to an hour we were forced to run around the camp, sometimes crawling, sometimes huddled together, while Germans, wearing bright green and red, randomly beat us with canes.

"I saw many people die from this 'sport' event; I also saw many comrades die from the beatings. During 1943 this 'sport' took place every other day." (83)

"During our stay in Auschwitz, 40 to 50 prisoners were killed for leaving the barracks during restricted periods." (71)

PRACTICES

"We women were not allowed to choose where we wanted to sleep; it was chosen for us. So we were mixed in with common criminals all of whom were mean and nasty." (12)

"We were in close contact with the most despicable, most dangerous people, all indiscriminately thrown together." (120)

"Furthermore, our women officers, some with peculiar propensities, had no qualms whatsoever about taking their pleasure with Gypsy women, who then received special treatment." (12)

"If they were pretty and healthy, the women and young girls were taken to a special barracks where the SS guards raped them until they were half dead. From there they were sent to the ovens." (101)

"There was a brothel that was reserved for prisoners who had been in the camp three years. To be admitted you had to have a permit from the camp doctor. The house was open only in the evening after roll call. An SS guard manned the entrance. In the morning the prostitutes, dressed in shorts, would perform military exercises while singing songs. In the evening a few select women would show up at the barracks of the SS." (17)

"Admission was 2 marks, of which the woman got 50 pfennigs. The rest (1.50 Reichmarks) went to organizations working for victory." (90)

"A certain number of Jews were retained in the camp for the use of the Kapos; the homosexual Kapos used them to gratify their lust and therefore protected them." (86)

RELIGION

"No kind of spiritual or moral support was allowed for the followers of any religion." (92)

"The presence of a priest would have done us much good, but it was strictly forbidden under threat of death for a priest to perform his office." (57)

"In all concentration camps every religious practice was forbidden under penalty of death.

"The overriding principle was to suppress anything that could remotely provoke thoughts of God; so under the pretext of disinfecting us, they confiscated our rosaries, which they threw in the trash, and also our holy pictures and medallions, many of which were keepsakes. Breviaries, missals, and other holy books were used for toilet paper." (90)

"I wanted to save a small holy picture, but one of the prisoners advised me not to try. He said it wasn't worth it, that they would only make fun of you and, in the end, take it away from you anyway." (104)

"I was accosted by a group of SS men who tore my soutane, broke my rosary, and with scornful sneers stomped on my breviary." (40)

"In our group were nuns whose clothes the Germans had gleefully thrown in the dirt." (85)

"Priestly clothes and accessories were turned into clothes for the prostitutes in the brothels.

"Since I was a priest and an Englishman, I was given additional work to do which consisted of scooping water out of a hole with a pail. I never succeeded in emptying the hole because it kept filling up again. I endured some bad moments. However, I was spared beatings and the hardest work, excavation.

"To find out if the faithful were saying their prayers, the SS relied on the Kapos. A professor of Oriental languages (Hebrew, Armenian, and Arabic) was killed by an orderly who heard him praying.

"One day several priests arrived at Auschwitz without registration numbers. They were disinfected and then quarantined. The next day, still wearing their soutanes, they were sent out to work at the railway station under the command of the head Kapo, who killed them before nightfall.

"In the summer of 1944 I did a postmortem on the leading Patriarch of the Orthodox Synod of Paris. Through the intercession of the International Red Cross, Stalin had allowed him to return to reorganize the orthodox church. Because of his rank and according to international law, this Patriarch, just like the Catholic Cardinals, had the right to move about freely and should never have been interned in the first place. When the Germans found out about Stalin's invitation, they apprehended the Patriarch and sent him to Buchenwald where he suffered severe stomach cramps. He had previously been operated on twice. He asked for a third operation and was turned down, but later they relented. As a result of this operation, he died a few days later." (90)

"We had a priest among us who was horribly mistreated. He was forced to kneel down, a brick in either hand, and say that Jesus Christ did not exist, that Hitler alone was Lord God Almighty. He didn't want to say it. Day in and day out he was kicked and beaten, even shot at, until finally he died." (50)

DAILY SCENES

"It was bitter cold. An SS guard told us (me and one of my comrades) to come into his barracks. He asked us if we were cold. We assured him we were. He told us he would warm us, and proceeded to knock our heads together. Then he asked us if we were still cold. We said no; and this time he spun us around, kicked us in the behind, and threw us out." (30)

"Once, after an SS guard had counted the prisoners in the cellblock, he cried: 'Fall out and wash up!' Nobody knew where to go, since no one had told us where the washrooms were. The first ones out ran in front of the barracks and were promptly greeted by two SS guards brandishing clubs. A lot of confusion ensued, what with those who were first out trying to get back in, while the others were trying to get out. (All of this was happening, by the way, in double-time.) Since we didn't know where we should go, our cellblock was in total chaos. We had barely got back inside when other SS guards drove us out with sharp kicks and blows from their clubs. Our guard, Z., stood in the middle of the passageway and, as the prisoners passed by, he struck them on their bare backs with a cane. Luckily we found the washroom. But scarcely had we started to wash up when we were ordered to fall out. Z. still stood in the passageway with his cane and tried, with a diabolical laugh, to strike each man who passed by. I remember only too well how a Belgian prisoner, who was 58 years old and severely weakened from two years confinement, received an especially severe blow. His red and blue welts were visible for a long time after that.

"When I arrived, the prisoners were in the process of building brick cellblocks. They had to haul the bricks from a place about a kilometer away from the camp. Each prisoner had to carry six bricks, quite a heavy load considering the distance and the weakened condition of most of the inmates. Once back in camp, we were supposed to place the bricks at the end of one of the barracks, but before we could put them down, we had to run all the way around the barracks still carrying the load. Two guards stood in our way, laughing and hitting each prisoner who passed.

"After we put the bricks down, we had to stack them in rows of three between the barracks. Unfortunately, the prisoners of Barracks 1 were standing by Barracks 2 and vice versa. When everything was ready, the order came to go inside. Immediately there was indescribable chaos. Those on the right had to run to the left, and those on the left had to run to the right. Many of them fell down, the others ran over them and, as usual, the guards pounced on us with their clubs, canes, boards, even their boots. I finally broke loose. As I entered the unlighted hallway of the barracks, I saw a bunch of people tangled up on the floor. Z. and another guard had placed two stools there so that the first to arrive would fall over them and those who followed would fall over the first. As usual, Z. and the other guards amused themselves by weighing in with some makeshift wooden clubs. A young Pole in our cell had the calf of his left leg half torn off.

"One after the other we had to enter the hallway of the barracks. Roughly 10 guards were lined up along its length. We were then ordered to run the length of the hallway three times, on our toes, with our hands behind our heads. The hallway was 150 feet long.

"Among us there were old people (over 60 years old), crippled people, and people who, after two years of imprisonment, had become emaciated and feeble. All of them were forced to hop up and down for no apparent reason. The hopping had barely begun when several of them could not hold out any longer. The guards pounced on the poor wretches and beat them with canes, with electric wires wrapped around their fists, with rifle butts, etc. I saw incredible acts of brutality. The aforementioned young Pole showed his wounded leg to SS Officer K., who took him aside in the latrine. As I passed by, I saw the young Pole crouched in a corner in front of K., who was viciously hitting and kicking him.

"A little later Z. returned and made us get in and out of bed repeatedly. After that he took the Frenchman M. aside and made him lie down and get back up twenty times. Why? M. was a Benedictine monk." (95)

"I went with SS Officer B. To a cell where a somewhat simple-minded young man was being held. When B. entered the cell, the young man did not stir from his place. B. exploded in a rage, grabbed the young man by the throat, pushed him against the bedstead, and kicked him mercilessly.

"Among the new arrivals was a young Frenchman who had been wounded in an air raid and was suffering from shell shock. He wanted to explain his case to someone and to let them know that he had been mistakenly locked up. Without a second thought B. started hitting him on the head. To protect himself from the blows, the young man held his arms in front of his face. B. struck him over and over again until the young man was bleeding so freely from his nose and his mouth that the blood spilled onto the floor. B. hit so hard and so often that the whole time I was there (9 weeks), his hands were greatly swollen and bandaged." (27)

"When a certain SS guard appeared in the streets of the camp, every internee warned his neighbor and they would all run and hide. He was a pervert who killed people for pleasure. The most likely to suffer were the Jews whom he especially hated. As soon as he found out that somewhere there would be a lot of them—for example, if he got a list of the new arrivals—he would hurry there and kill a bunch of them. He was also a sex maniac who satisfied his lust with young Jewish girls, whom he murdered immediately afterwards." (90)

"SS Officer H. became enraged at me one day and hit me repeatedly in the face, but I stood motionless before him.

"'Shame on you, striking an unarmed man,' I said. 'There is no heroism in attacking a man who has no weapon.'

"H. became even more infuriated and screamed: 'I am a German and you are only a pig Jew, and you dare to tell me to my face that I ought to be ashamed?'

"The more he screamed, the higher his voice got. He spied a board in front of him, took it, threw it at me, hitting me in the head with it. I fell to the floor, my head gushing blood.

"'Shame, shame on all of you,' I cried. 'The more you hit me, the greater is your shame.'

"I felt that the end was near. He hit me again. Nothing could save me. Suddenly the board dropped from his hands. He flung himself at me and went on beating me on the head.

"I made it back to camp with a great deal of effort and went as soon as I could to the office of Gauleiter B. to complain about H. B. was one of the few 'mortal enemies' who was not malicious. He felt sorry for me but admitted that it would be impossible for him to act on my complaint and lodge an official reprimand against H., for H. had an important position in the Nazi party and, therefore, more influence than B., who, although a Gauleiter, was not a member of the party. I had no choice but to back off.

"Fifteen minutes later Camp Commander U. came for me personally and took me to his room. I knew immediately what was going to happen in the next few moments. The captain of the guards also entered the room.

"U. began without hesitation: 'You have had the impudence to complain about H. You should know first of all that complaints are supposed to be sent to *me*. Furthermore, you should know that I pay no attention whatsoever to the complaints of a Jew. Jews have done so much evil that all of them should be hanged without delay. Every piece of bread they are given is too much; it is stealing from the German people. And now for my answer.' With that, he came at me and began hitting me in the face until I fell to the floor.

"With great effort I stood up, but now it was the captain of the guards' turn to rough me up. He knocked me to the floor with a hammer blow to the head, screaming: 'Now, you Schweinehund, you pig Jew, you piece of filth, you won't be insulting any more Germans, not if you think back on this day.'" (34)

"In order to acquaint us with camp discipline, they assembled us (old and new we numbered about 15,000) in the place where two prisoners were being hanged to the sound of music." (58)

"One real Nazi fanatic took a shot at every prisoner he saw on the street simply for the fun of doing it. There was nothing to be done about him because he was the liaison officer, and he defended his actions on the grounds that, since the prisoner was trying to escape, he had squelched resistance and put himself in great danger doing it. In this way he managed to kill thousands of prisoners." (90)

"A 'green' German prisoner, who held the office of foreman in the mines, had established relations with a German woman who also worked in the mines. He wrote to this woman, and she wrote back. One day a letter fell into the hands of S. That evening at roll call he told the foreman to step forward and said to him: 'Ah, you are drunk with love; I will empty you out.' The man had to strip naked and run around the parade ground, stopping every 50 yards to masturbate at gunpoint.

"A load of prisoners arrived from Fresnes made up of Jews and Englishmen. Upon their arrival, the Jews were forced to wade fully clothed through a trough filled with water five feet deep. To 'dry off,' they were ordered to empty the latrine using only a wheelbarrow and a spoon.

"We were told that at the slightest hint of discontent, machine guns would open fire on us immediately. At the same time, the camp leader made a high-minded speech in which he told us that if we were surprised to be in our present situation, we had only the Jews to blame." (17)

"We watched as some prisoners were tied hand and foot and forced to hop around the basin. The SS guards struck the ones who couldn't go any farther or fell and couldn't get up fast enough." (42)

"In the morning we performed these exercises for up to four hours or until we couldn't go on." (31)

"I could not do these exercises because one of the guards—who was 63, my own age!—kept beating me. " (31)

"The next day I had to perform frog jumps for half an hour. After that, the SS guard forced me to jump on the bed and then crawl underneath it, jump up on the table and then crawl underneath it, and crawl under the chairs and then climb on top the wardrobe He acted like he was going to shoot me, forced me to pretend I was preaching, then had me climb down, then back up again, and finally made me sing hymns for two hours.

"Whenever I was unable to complete my gymnastics, I was kicked and beaten." (90)

"One morning two soldiers forced two French prisoners who had gotten sick from daily beatings to eat the excrement encrusted in their clothing. They made these two prisoners walk up and down the mess hall telling their fellow prisoners how good it tasted." (11)

"One SS guard ordered his dog to bite a deportee and when it didn't obey, the guard hit the dog so hard it vomited; whereupon an Israeli was ordered to eat the dog's vomit." (39)

"Once in Mauthausen a 16-year-old Spanish boy came to me full of fear and I told him to stay. A guard came into the room, approached me, and ordered me to do something which I refused to do. He made as if to hit me. The Spanish boy, who was hiding under the bed, thought that the guard was going to ask me where the boy was, so he ran out of the barracks and straight into the electrified barbed-wire fence. The guard gave an order, and right before my very eyes the boy was torn apart by eight vicious dogs." (89)

"One of the SS guards, a 19-year-old boy, acted as overseer of the prisoners who were working on the construction of an improved crematory. He approached one of the strongest and best-looking workers, ordered him to bow his head, and struck him full force on the back of the neck with his cudgel. As the worker collapsed, the SS guard ordered two prisoners to take him by the legs and, with his face to the ground, swing him around in an effort to revive him. After they had lugged him across 100 yards of frozen earth, he had still not regained consciousness and remained motionless. So the SS guard grabbed a cement sewer pipe, lifted it up, and brought it down on the back of the victim who was already lying unconscious on the ground. This he did five times. At the first blow, the body of the victim twitched in death throes; at the second blow it grew stiff. At the fifth blow the guard ordered the victim to be turned faced up, and then he pried his eyelids open with a stick. When he had made sure that the man was dead, the guard spat on him, lit a cigarette, and then walked away as if nothing had happened." (110)

"Frequently the SS guards would storm into our barracks in the middle of the night, drive us naked outside no matter how bad the weather, and make us crawl, run, whatever. Those who did not perform fast enough or showed signs of weakening were thrashed to death." (22)

"We were scarcely across the threshold before they began hitting on the head all those who tried to slip by them. To speed up the process, they turned the dogs loose and let them attack us and bite us. One after the other, they made us go in and out repeatedly just to train the dogs." (17)

"They would drag an internee up before a gleaming white mangle and force him to stick his finger between the two large rubber cylinders. Then an SS guard or, at his command, a prisoner would turn the crank of the mangle. The arm of the victim would then be squeezed up to the elbow or the shoulder. The screams of the victim were the chief amusement of the SS guards. Meanwhile, the man whose arm had been crushed was relegated to the category of the disabled and summarily condemned to death.

"One of their 'ingenious amusements' was the following: An SS guard would collar a few prisoners and tell them that they had broken some camp rule or other and that they were to be shot. One of the prisoners would then be stood against the wall, and the guard would press his revolver against the prisoner's temple. Expecting to be shot, 99 times out of 100 the victim would close his eyes. Then the guard would shoot into the air while another guard would stealthily sneak up on the victim and give him a severe blow on the head with a huge board. The prisoner would then collapse unconscious. When, after a few minutes, he would come to and open his eyes, the guard who was standing beside him would say, laughing wildly: 'You see, you're in the hereafter. You see also that in the hereafter there are Germans. It's impossible to escape us.' Since the prisoner would be bleeding profusely and not have the power to stand up, he was considered as good as dead, and after the guards had had their fun with him, they would shoot him.

"Another 'amusement': A prisoner would be stripped and thrown into the swimming pool. He would try to stay afloat and somehow get out of the water. Meanwhile, the SS guards would be scrambling around the pool, doing their best to push or kick him away from the edge. If he did manage to avoid their kicks, he had the right to climb out of the water, but only on condition that he get completely dressed again in three seconds. The guards stood there timing this with their watches in their hands. Naturally, no one could possibly get dressed in three seconds, so the victim would be thrown back into the water where he would eventually drown.

"At nine o'clock in the morning on December 2, 1941, the prisoners were assembled and told that a packet of tobacco had been stolen from a supervisor and that the offender should return it at once. All the prisoners insisted that they did not have the tobacco, and then the Nazi brutes began their little game. Everybody was ordered to undress. The temperature was about 15 degrees above zero. Nobody resisted because everyone knew that to do so would be suicide, so all they could do was wait and see what would happen to 500 naked people.

"At midday the first ones collapsed, some beaten to death, others unconscious. They tried to arouse the unconscious by whipping them, but none of them could stand up again and they all died, their backs broken. A lot of the other prisoners got pneumonia and high fevers. When the brutes noticed this, they said: 'Oh, are you overheated? Good. We'll cool you off.' The sick were then thrown into bathtubs filled with icy water, and when they lost consciousness, they either drowned or were taken straight from the bathtub and thrown into a cement cell where these poor wretches would crawl around on the floor seeking the warm body of a comrade who himself would perish the next minute. One of these wretches tried warming his fingers in the nostrils of a comrade. The jailers would measure those who were still alive for their coffins, then remind them of their impending death and stamp a number on their thighs. In this one night 32 died." (96)

"When they felt the urge, the Nazis would fire from the shooting range, mowing down everything that appeared in the main street of the camp, or they would fire into the barracks without warning when they heard too much noise, or maybe 30 brutes with clubs or revolvers in their fists would strike out right and left. The inmates would jump out the windows and, pressed by those behind them, get entangled in the electric fence six feet away." (50)

"Some of us were driven crazy." (98)

"Without any reason whatsoever, the Kapos would call us out, one after the other, just to beat us. Those of us who didn't succumb to the beatings were kicked." (33)

"In Block 21 we took care of a great many prisoners suffering from fractured jaws they got from being beaten by the Kapos." (86)

"Somewhere around 80 percent of those who were admitted to the hospital died a few days later." (87)

"Some of my fellow prisoners died because a Kapo wanted to show someone how you could kill a person with just one blow." (43)

"The internees who had been common criminals were the worst (Polish or German). They would kill a Jew just for his bread or his soup. One 18 year-old Kapo killed more than 400 Jews for their food rations." (100)

"We were herded into the latrine single file. A Kapo stood at the door. No sooner were we inside the lavatory than the Kapo would begin to count in a loud voice. He would count to 10, and by then you had to be out again. If you couldn't make it in that time, you risked being hit on the head with a blow intended to be fatal. Every day many of my friends died as a result of a visit to the latrine." (101)

"The head Kapo at the train station at Auschwitz had killed 30,000 prisoners in order to attain his freedom and be accepted into Hitler's Life Guards." (90)

"Women suffered the same fate. They were beaten and abused. The mortality rate was higher for them than it was for men." (104)

"M. planned to carry out the sentence of 25 blows with a rubber truncheon on three Jewish women who had been caught eating raw turnips while unloading a freight car. The carrying out of this punishment was horrible: the women cried out, it was unbearable. M. ordered his soldiers to pick up the ones who had fallen to the ground and hit them again.

"Another time the women had been laughing and singing on their way back from the factory. M. ordered them to stand for an hour and a half in snow up to their knees and with an icy wind blowing.

"And yet another time, when the women had laughed, he put them in two rows, grabbed a whip made of five or six knotted ropes, and hit them across the face with it. For the slightest infraction we were deprived of food for two whole days." (55)

"B. came to the camp on a bicycle. Along the way he knocked the prisoners about, went out of his way to pick on the the elderly, and boxed ears on the slightest provocation." (53)

"I saw SS matrons beat a friend of mine senseless with a leather belt." (61)

"There was one SS matron, a common criminal (she had murdered her husband), who was especially brutal. She kicked and beat many of the female prisoners mercilessly, and once, when I turned around to look at a friend of mine, she gave me a vicious blow to the head and kicked me in the stomach." (97)

"We called her the 'green mare' because of her protruding teeth. She knew only too well how to belt you in the mouth hard enough to knock your teeth out or break your jaw. One day the 'green mare' struck me with her fist because my shoelaces were untied.

"There was another SS matron who was constantly threatening us with her revolver; we called her the 'animal trainer.' Another we called the 'boar.' All these women were products of the Hitler Youth and had been thoroughly indoctrinated. They themselves had been woefully abused." (28)

"Often the SS matrons would amuse themselves by displays of appalling brutality in their dealings with the female internees. One evening they summoned an internee to their 'studio' and an SS matron knocked her down the minute she got there. Then another, who was short, climbed up on a table so that she could reach the internee's breast with her feet and gave them a powerful kick." (72)

"The one we called 'Lageracerca' was a scrawny, repulsive old battle-ax. She stood out because of her sadism and her sexual perversity; she was half crazy. At either the morning or the evening roll call she would search among the exhausted and emaciated women for the prettiest, those who more or less still looked human, and would whack them on the hands for no reason whatsoever. If the victims collapsed, the 'Lageracerca' would go for their legs, first with her whip, then with her spiked boots. Usually her victims left a bloody trail behind them, and after one or two such mistreatments would soon turn sick and die." (110)

"One woman was sentenced to death after she was denounced by a German internee for giving water to a Jewish woman." (77)

"When we first got to the camp, there were 120 of us women. A month later 30 were dead." (61)

"Many times the Block leader was ordered to kill a certain number of women. These women were beaten until they passed out. I myself saw the camp strewn with bodies; they looked like white seagulls lying prostrate in the snow." (103)

ROLL CALL

"Whether it rained, or snowed, or stormed—in fog or in sunshine—all prisoners had to fall out for roll call every morning." (74)

"They woke us up at 3:30 in the morning." (116)

"If you happened to stretch out in bed for even another minute, you'd be rousted out with a billy club and doused with cold water." (120)

"Sick women were not excused from this 'martyrdom' called roll call; I say 'martyrdom,' because I saw many women pass out from the cold, from standing in the snow with an icy wind blowing. Since you had to have a temperature of over 100 degrees to be admitted to the hospital, you can well imagine what an unbearable wait that meant for a prisoner who had only a 99-degree temperature and who had been brutally torn from, if not a warm bed, then at least a lukewarm one. The female guards, 'lady soldiers,' who were inhumane to us, admitted without shame that the purpose of such treatment was to hasten our extermination. Once I fainted from weakness and by sheer accident came to again without any help." (42)

"Often I even had to assist comrades to roll call who had passed out or were suffering an epileptic fit. We had to lay them next to us on the ground and were not allowed to take care of them. I got a lot of blows

Bodies stacked like firewood might wait weeks to be disposed of

Vicious guard dogs (right) and diabolical instruments of torture (below) were commonplace methods of discipline and punishment

Prisoners were frequently forced to stand roll call naked for hours on end, in all kinds of weather

A rare, sunny day mocks the mire and filth, not to mention the monotony and menace of daily life in the camps

One spigot often had to serve thousands of prisoners

from fists and clubs from the German or Polish policewomen or female guards because I tried to help women who were writhing in the dirt in an epileptic fit." (67)

"At the first roll call a friend of mine was sick. Naively, I went up to our 'Blockova' and said: 'Excuse me for bothering you, but a friend of mine is very sick, can she be excused from roll call?' She answered: 'Here even the dying come to roll call.'" (28)

"As a matter of fact, not only the dying but those who had died that day had to attend roll call so that the figures jibed. They were laid out on a bench that was carried by two prisoners." (64)

"Three times I had to prop up dead bodies at roll call. Finally, I told an SS guard that this didn't make any sense. His answer was: 'Dead or alive, everybody has to be there.' Then he added: 'Roll call is roll call.'" (54)

"Every morning the dead and the dying were dragged to roll call." (60)

"There was a child with us about six months old. This child had to come with us to roll call, but of course it had to be carried in someone's arms, and that ruined the symmetry of the lineup. An SS guard decided, therefore, that the child should be 'posted' to a brothel. 'Posted' ordinarily referred to those deportees who were distributed among the various inner circles of the camp. They enjoyed preferential treatment that excused them from roll call on account of their work. The SS guard added that the child would be taken care of in a more motherly fashion. I asked why the child was being taken into custody and was told: 'For the good of the Greater Reich.'

"If a comrade did not show up for roll call, we had to stay there as long as the search for him lasted." (54)

"In Mauthausen I saw the way one Russian comrade, who was five minutes late for roll call, was kicked in the head by twelve SS guards." (39)

"Rabbi E., who suffered from dysentery, met a tragic end one day when he was a few minutes late for roll call. The squad leader grabbed hold of him and plunged his head into the toilet and poured cold water on him; then he took out a revolver and shot him." (104)

"We stood roll call for up to five and a half hours, while the weak were stretched out on the ground in front of the 'lady officers.' Speaking was forbidden unless you wanted a bucket of water over your head, and the mornings were cold." (116)

"The Kapo of our unit killed a friend of mine because he was not standing up straight. He hit him on the jaw with his fist, and when my my friend had fallen to the ground, he choked him by pressing his foot down on his throat." (33)

"Evening roll call often lasted so long that the poor prisoners had to endure the harsh Polish climate for hours on end." (60)

"Ravensbrück concentration camp was built on a drained swamp. The earth there was so acidic that it caused bad burns. Many had their legs half eaten away. Out in the open country, the acid in the air clawed at your face and caused the skin to fester. Women who had been there for a long time had horrible sores. I couldn't bear to look at them." (76)

"After 12 hours' work and a roll call at 6 p.m., the whole camp would sometimes be called out to the parade ground for another roll call at midnight, a particularly unpleasant experience on bitterly cold winter nights.

"During snowstorms there were seemingly endless roll calls day and night. We had to stand there for three, sometimes four, even six hours." (63)

"At the time of the German defeat at Stalingrad, we had an especially long roll call. It took place during a snowstorm and lasted all day long. The next day the roll call continued." (14)

"1,200 standing in formation, motionless and numb with cold." (63)

"The first shock I received at a night roll call was hearing a passing SS guard ask the squad leader: 'How many dead?' 'Ten,' answered the squad leader. To which the guard responded: 'What, so few?'" (35)

"As a matter of fact, most of the prisoners died at roll call." (103)

"Many of my comrades perished at the morning roll call. I saw at least one die each day, and frequently as many as three." (74)

"If you were unconscious and could not respond at roll call, your name was put on a list of the dead and you would be clubbed to death." (111)

"Sometimes six or seven people would drop dead at roll call, in addition to countless other prisoners who had to be taken to the infirmary, which was filled with the dying. Often ten would fall dead, but you didn't dare move them. That was forbidden." (63)

"People collapsed. Sometimes the dogs were turned loose on them to make sure they were dead." (14)

"The SS guards, armed with rubber truncheons, overwhelmed them with blows and kicks to make them stand up, which was impossible, since they were already dead." (74)

"A Belgian minister died during a roll call that took place in extraordinarily cold weather." (62)

PUNISHMENT AND TORTURE

"Routine punishments were: 25 lashes on the buttocks with a cane or a whip; several hours standing motionless in the summer sun or half naked in freezing temperatures; 2 or 3 days of starvation; running for half an hour carrying a 40 pound stone past a line of guards who took turns whipping the prisoners as they passed by." (92)

"The most frequent punishment was caning." (10)

"For the slightest infraction, prisoners would be caned or beaten with a whip." (96)

"The SS guards ordered us to bend over and stick our heads and shoulders between two posts which they immediately clamped tightly together. When you are held fast like that, you are no longer in control of your movements. And while you are struggling in vain to get free, somebody is giving you 25 lashes from behind." (101)

"For the slightest disobedience, you'd get a minimum of 25 lashes from the SS." (21)

"The number of lashes varied according to the gravity of the transgression (25, 50, 100)." (96)

"Collective punishment usually took the form of starving the whole camp for anywhere from three to, as was often the case, eight days. (In November 1939 this punishment was made worse for the Jews by locking them up in blacked-out barracks.) During this time the prisoners were forced to stand at attention in freezing temperatures. One time this punishment lasted six days, by the end of which 180 prisoners had died. Of 12,000 camp inmates, at least ten percent died as a result of these measures. It was the worst torture in the camp. Other punishments included disciplinary drills after working hours. Prisoners disciplined in this way usually died." (105)

"Of all the cellblocks, one block was much worse than the others: the 'punishment block.'" (46)

"This dungeon was in total darkness and built so that the prisoners in it could neither lie down nor stand up straight." (107)

"Whether alone or in groups, the women prisoners had to stand ankle deep in water." (53)

"The occupants of the dungeon didn't get any food." (107)

"During your stay in the dungeon you would be sentenced to receive a minimum of 25 lashes per day. An SS guard would beat you with a bullwhip; the pain was unbearable." (120)

"For the most part the beatings were applied to the small of the back, which would lacerate your flesh." (21)

"A wound might measure six inches in diameter on either half of the buttocks, which meant that the two halves were nothing but one big wound." (80)

"Beatings were usually accompanied by other measures. One internee was led into the shower stall and left to hang for a couple of hours with his hands tied behind his back. During this time he was severely beaten in the face and all over his body with a bullwhip. When he was brought back to the office of the liaison officer, he had to sign a statement. Then he was forced to stand at attention from 10 o'clock one morning until 7 the next. Another internee, along with two of his friends, was taken to the shower stalls. There he was given 25 lashes on the buttocks and lower back with a wet bullwhip. As with the others who were punished, he was forced to count the number of lashes. If one of those being beaten made a mistake in counting, the two SS guards would begin the punishment all over from the beginning. After receiving the 25 lashes, the internee was forced to perform strenuous calisthenics until the other two had received their punishment.

"If one of the victims didn't do the exercises properly or happened to stumble, he would be beaten severely with the bullwhip on every imaginable part of his body. One of the two prisoners being punished with H. was a Jew who was beaten to death by the SS guards; the other prisoners were forced to carry the corpse to the dungeon. H., along with the two other prisoners (one of whom was dead), was locked up for three days and nights in the dungeon. He was obliged to remain standing because his wounds made it impossible for him to sit or lie down." (107)

"I myself was horribly mistreated. My head was so swollen from frequent beatings that nobody recognized me any more. R. M., director of the outpatient clinic of the camp hospital and the one who bandaged me, can attest to the condition I was in when I appeared before him after that kind of treatment. In this condition I had to take off my stockings, arrange my clothes in perfect order, and quickly unbutton my jacket, all of which caused me such excruciating pain that my limbs refused to function." (38)

"If a prisoner, from total exhaustion, could no longer do what was demanded of her, she was considered a 'backslider' and locked in a cell without food until she died." (113)

"The prisoners were constantly tortured." (112)

"I saw one woman whose head one torturer immersed in a tub of water until she lost consciousness; then this fiend brought her to by hitting her on the head with his fists." (42)

"I suffered the following torture: stuck with red-hot pins all over my body, total dislocation of both legs which resulted in torn ligaments. Scars from these various tortures were still quite visible nine months later, particularly one ugly scar on my thigh which was the result of a stab wound. At the time I was tortured, I was forced to undress; then two women were called over to take a look at me, for it had been maintained that all priests had syphilis and they wanted to prove it. It was up to us to prove that it was not true. One of the most painful ordeals I ever had to endure was having tufts of facial hair pulled out by the roots." (54)

"My fingers were crushed in a device especially designed for that purpose; then I was stuck into a barrel-shaped wooden contraption in which my body was crushed by a steel disk. I was not released until I began to spit gall and blood." (72)

"I was hung by the thumbs and beaten on the feet; my head was immersed in water and my private parts stuck with needles. My back was tied to a barrel while someone pulled at my limbs and tried to tear them apart." (20)

"T. had one eye gouged out and his fingernails and toenails torn off. The brothers F. were grotesquely kicked and beaten until they passed out from dislocated limbs and were thrown in the cellar. For two days they remained unconscious. They were in such a delirium that one of them invited me to accompany him to a café and a ball. They had gone mad. They vomited and urinated blood." (119)

"On March 21, I saw five Alsatians, one hand chained to the wall, the other behind their back; they remained like that for four or five days because they didn't want to fight for Germany." (85)

"Often they fastened the hands of the accused behind their backs with handcuffs and let them hang by their wrists from the ceiling, all the while beating them with a whip. Some passed out, others went crazy and began to sing." (25)

"They committed the following atrocities: They would fasten your wrists with loose handcuffs, stick your knees in the oval that was formed, and then push a stick between the back of your knees and the inside of your elbows, forming a ball. You would then be stood on your head with your knees and one of your shoulders serving as a base. This position was eventually attained with the help of kicks and blows. Two men would then take sticks and beat you with all their might on the back, the buttocks, and the ankles. I myself once counted 187 blows. When the pain got so bad that the victims could no longer keep from screaming, the torturers would take the victims aside and stamp on their faces with their hobnailed boots while an 'assistant' would stuff their mouths with rags." (119)

"My hands became paralyzed after I had been hanging for hours by my handcuffs." (80)

"The torture was so bad that Colonel B. went on a hunger strike. He died about one month after our arrival." (8)

"The instruments of torture included handcuffs with serrated pincers, apparatuses for crushing the genitals, and bullwhips with lead studs at the tips. They knew just how far they could go and still leave their victims alive, which is why their victims often preferred death. When the parts of the body that were normally abused became immune to pain, they would go for the more sensitive parts, like the genitals.

"S., a 35-year-old father, was abused in a way that comes close to being the ultimate refinement in gruesomeness. When he got back from the first treatment, he no longer had the strength to stand, and the gaping wounds on his body did not permit him to lie down. These brutes had crushed his penis and his testicles." (119)

"My penis was subjected to electric shock by means of a device that had the precision of a fine, surgical instrument. It consisted of a tube made out of two flexible steel bands connected at the end and fitted with a ring and a screw. They stuck your penis in and tightened the screw. At the end of the tube was a wire that led to a rheostat. When the current was turned on, you felt absolutely nothing. The pain was triggered when the current was interrupted, causing sharp jolts to be sent to the nerves." (88)

"The wife of the Kommandant used to go riding every day. If she caught an internee looking at her, she would make a note of his number. The internee would immediately be thrown into prison, given 25 blows with a club, and sometimes killed." (38)

"When the jailer conducted an interrogation, he would carry his revolver and threaten to shoot any prisoner who did not confess. Not surprisingly, he sometimes shot a prisoner." (65)

"One prisoner was kept in a cellar, blindfolded and chained, for six months." (117)

"Once the number of those being tortured reached about 30 people. The more wine and schnapps they got for their effort, the more wanton the SS guards became. In the adjacent dormitory the internees could not close their eyes the whole night because of the anguished cries of the tortured. The ordeal lasted until morning roll call and was such that most of the victims could no longer stand up. The were badly cut up. Many of them were unrecognizable from having been beaten in the face.

"For four weeks the tortured were exposed to the rigors of the weather, their hands always tied behind their backs, except when they had to use the bathroom or eat or drink. The chains were so heavy that the sufferers began to complain. Finally they were hanged." (25)

"Many internees died in the camp as a result of relentless torture." (107)

"Many were whipped until they died. Many were strangled. Many were drained completely of their blood." (56)

"During the 13 months I was in jail, 300 to 400 deportees were murdered. I can give you a fairly exact number because those who carried the bodies would call out at the entrance whenever an internee had been murdered." (38)

"Almost no one got out of the camp prisons alive." (105)

"To look out the cell windows meant certain death. Internees who happened to get caught were beaten, stabbed, or murdered. The same punishment awaited those who even glanced at a piece of newspaper (especially when it was intended to be used as toilet paper)." (38)

"Instances of hangings for trivial things (stealing bread or stealing wire for shoelaces) were frequent. Such was the fate of two French prisoners." (22)

"The camp was fenced in by two narrowly separated rows of electrified barbed wire which also provided an opportunity for punishment. Those being punished had to spend the night between the two rows of wire, close to a watchtower, where they could neither lie down nor sit; they had had to remain standing and, of course, got nothing to eat. When their exhaustion brought them to the point where they could no longer hold out, they would stumble against one or the other of the electrified fences and be found dead." (90)

"Another favorite method the Nazis had for torturing prisoners was stringing them up from trees. During 1938/39 this form of torture was common in the forests surrounding the camp. 20 to 25 trees were selected for this purpose and were equipped with hooks six feet up the trunk. The hands of the prisoners would be tied behind their backs and they would be hoisted up until their feet no longer touched the ground. The camp leader and an SS guard would go from tree to tree and beat the prisoners with a whip. The shortest hanging time was half an hour. To be left hanging there for three hours was not uncommon. This torture was performed at least twice a week.

"20 prisoners were chained together and forced to form a circle around a tree in the camp courtyard. All night long the SS sicced their dogs on them. By morning only three prisoners were still alive." (105)

"One SS guard hanged a prisoner from a branch and then forced the prisoner's comrades to use the branch to catapult the body into midair so that he could take potshots at it." (70)

"The specialty of another one of the 'torturer's apprentices' was to drown prisoners in a barrel. The SS guards would grab hold of a man by the legs, plunge him into a barrel of icy water, pull him out, then repeat this procedure over and over again until the man drowned." (95)

"A Polish priest was publicly castrated. After this operation, the priest was bandaged with a towel and returned, with the help of his comrades, to his quarters where he was drowned." (90)

"I was witness to the following scene: One poor prisoner, after he had been viciously beaten, was dragged into a washroom (March 1944, washroom of Block 48), laid on the ground, and doused with buckets of cold water until he died." (3)

"A few days after our arrival, the Block leader killed one of our comrades from Bordeaux in a horrible way. He first made him strip naked, then drenched him in cold water and left him outside for several hours (it was the first of February), then he was brought back inside the Block and tied to a post. The next morning, about 5 o'clock, he received a beating that broke his neck, and when he didn't die quickly enough, the orderlies submerged his head in a bucket of dirty dishwater." (8)

"An SS woman killed a little French girl by forcing her to drink water until she couldn't swallow any more. Then she knocked her down and tried using the heel of her boots to force the girl to vomit up the water. She hit her so hard that the girl vomited blood." (48)

"After endless torment the prisoners no longer had the strength to cover the 30 feet required to get back in line. Those who remained lying on the floor were taken to the camp kennels where they became the main course for the ravenous German shepherds. With their sharp teeth these vicious dogs tore apart the bodies of people who had been thrown into the cages still half alive. We found out later that whatever scraps of human flesh were left over from this feeding frenzy were taken daily to the crematory. No trace was left. Everything was spotless, even pleasant." (110)

"To every act of horror a certain number of prisoners were required to be present as observers. In this death camp the cries of pain were sometimes so excruciating that the Kommandant, thinking he was doing something to alleviate the suffering, had the prisoners who were not serving as observers gather together on a hill not far from the place of torture and sing uplifting songs." (96)

"On the iron gate itself you could read the motto of the camp: 'JEDEM DAS SEINE' ('To Each His Own')." (69)

"Jedem Das Seine" ("To Each His Own")—the cruelly ironic welcome to one of the camps

Electrified barbed wire stretches along a restraining canal at this camp hidden in the foothills of a scenic mountain range

A grim tableau of utter hopelessness

Chapter 6

Labor

MEN AT WORK

"The central administration of the camp had contractual obligations with German firms such as Krupp, Kohlen-Syndikat, etc., which a certain number of worker-prisoners had to fulfill." (86)

"All prisoners were obliged to work." (60)

"Without exception: men, women, old people, young people, pregnant women, the sick." (125)

"The fact that I was a medical student did not stop them from putting me to work as a bricklayer, farm worker, miner, or electrician." (81)

"The deportees were made available for work at the Gustloff factory, which belonged to finance minister Sauckel, the Mibau factory (radio-electronic war supplies), the D.A.W., etc.

"The following departments were established in the Gustloff factory:

Finishing and assembling weapons, with 280 prisoners, on February 23, 1944. Factory 11 on April 1, 1943, with 51 prisoners, a number which grew to 300. Following its destruction in an air raid, 1,500 prisoners were transferred to the cleaning up of four warehouses. The von Mibau factory began cleaning up operations in November 1943 with 30 prisoners; by November 1944 there were 1,500. After the raid, only 30 prisoners were assigned to cleaning up.

"The list of the war supply facilities that continued to use prison labor is as follows:

Munitions factory: Oberndorf	200	prisoners
Gustloff: Weimar	2,252	prisoners
Aircraft factories: Erla and Leipzig	948	prisoners

Artillery factories: Hasag, Leipzig, and Taucha	825	prisoners
Junker factories: various cities	5,875	prisoners
BMW factories: Eisenach and Abderoda	619	prisoners
Aircraft factory Siebel: Halle	633	prisoners
Bochum Syndicate	1,167	prisoners
Hasaag: various cities	3,609	prisoners
Rhine Metal Borsig: Düsseldorf	260	prisoners
Brown Coal Gasoline, A.G.: Magdeburg-Troglitz	3,828	prisoners
Military garages		Construction squads
SS-Home		Farm squads
Quarries		Plumbing squads
Masonry		SS city squads

"All of these squads had been in operation since the camp opened. Their continuation depended on that of the camp. In October 1942, Squad X supplied farm workers for the Gusloff factory. In 1943, the railroad between Weimar and Buchenwald was built by about 1,000 prisoners." (71)

"Other workers were put to work building underground factories for the construction of the V 1 rocket, building new facilities in the camp, unloading airplane motors in the middle of the forest, and laying water pipes. They also built streets that led to the forest. All work of this kind was done far from civilian population centers.

"We also worked for the I. G. Farben Industry, which employed approximately 40,000 civilians: Poles, Ukrainians, French, etc., plus 10,000 camp inmates and 400 to 500 English prisoners-of-war." (125)

"There was in addition a so-called 'cable wire' department that made steel nets for snaring submarines. The work consisted of rolling out very stiff, unextruded steel wire, which was very rough and tore the hands of the workers. In this department there was tremendous pressure for increased output. I also had to work in the optical department where prisoners polished lenses for a German war goods factory. This work was done in air thick with a gas—I think it was tetrachloride—which induced a kind of asthma that afflicted many of my comrades. Mostly Belgians were used in this department, but there were also a few French workers." (52)

"On the afternoon of July 22, 1944, 1,400 French workers were sent to join the work crews in Neckarelz and Neckargerach. Both these crews were stationed in Neckartal, 12 miles southeast of Heidelberg. They supplied manpower for various undertakings, in particular: outfitting an underground aircraft factory in Obrigheim, outfitting a similar factory in Hochhausen, building barracks for the disciplining of SS personnel, building barracks for the homeless, and performing certain farming tasks in the area." (92)

"For example, the airstrip at Klein Königsberg was built by 300 deportees who leveled the ground by tamping it down with their feet for days on end. By the time this job was done, only 10 of them were left." (114)

"During the first few months several squads were sent out to dig ditches along the Dutch and Danish borders. Many prisoners worked at unloading cargo boats." (63)

"In the fields we worked like horses pulling heavy wagons full of potatoes. We loaded them up and brought them in." (21)

"Finally there were the so-called 'heavy stone carriers.' They had to lift heavy stones up to their shoulders and then heave them onto a wagon. The foremen would not allow two men to help each other with a stone." (64)

"Awakened at 3:30 in the morning! A few minutes later roll call would begin, which meant standing at attention until 6. Work began at 6:30. Before they were marched out to work, everyone was carefully searched. Those internees in prison clothes were lined up in columns of three and surrounded by guards with rifles and machine guns." (121)

"The march to work was accompanied by the sound of cheerful music. The orchestra was made up of musicians who were true artists." (103)

"So, forward in military step and start out on the left foot!" (18)

"We had to run the whole way." (121)

"A lot of the prisoners had to cover a good five miles to the work zone." (78)

"We were forced to sing along the way. Whoever did not sing would be severely beaten. We also had to march with our shoes on our shoulders so as not to wear them out." (33)

"A big, empty truck and a few stretcher bearers followed. Anybody who got out of line or collapsed from exhaustion was shot on the spot and loaded onto the truck by the bearers. In the evening, the truck never came back empty." (121)

"In winter we worked 11 hours straight in snow up to our knees." (59)

"Fires were lit at which the Kapos warmed themselves, but the workers, of course, had no access to them. In temperatures of 10 to 20 below zero they had to handle iron products; naturally most of them suffered frostbitten hands." (87)

"I remember particularly the case of an American named R. who worked with us for just a week before he died of exposure." (79)

"After a few weeks of this sort of work, a terrible epidemic of typhus broke out. The weakest prisoners died by the hundreds." (104)

"In the railroad tunnel we worked in intolerable dust. There was no real ventilation. Whatever air there was came from two openings in the tunnel three kilometers apart, and it was contaminated by the soot from the trains, the machinery in the tunnel, and, above all, the blasting.

"The work consisted of unloading rails and machinery brought into the tunnel by train on a track that ran the entire length of the tunnel. The material was unloaded at alcoves dug into the sides of the tunnel. Other prisoners were assigned to work in the shafts." (7)

"The prisoners lived in the mine, in alcoves dug into the tunnel walls in which wooden frames with four floors had been installed. It was almost impossible to sleep." (108)

"The farm work was difficult and dangerous. In the first few months workers lost more than 50 pounds, which, of course, they could never gain back." (43)

"Elsewhere, the work consisted of carrying stones and loading them onto a small railroad car, all done under the following conditions: Two prisoners had to load a car in ten minutes. Then they had to push the car 100 yards ahead so it could be hooked onto a locomotive. It has been estimated that at least 50,000 prisoners lost their lives at this job." (75)

"Deportees who worked in an underground stone quarry in Linz went one whole year without seeing the light of day." (117)

"The work was often senseless. It consisted of lugging heavy stones from one end of the quarry to the other and from the bottom to the top and then back again—always in double time." (75)

"The Germans had countless groups of professors, doctors, engineers, and other professionals from Greece doing common labor, like hauling heavy stones, that far exceeded their strength. The SS beat to death those scholars who collapsed in exhaustion from the hard work. The whole group of Greek scholars was eliminated inside of five weeks by a system of starvation, debilitating work, beatings, and murder." (111)

"Nobody could withstand that sort of punishment." (104)

"A Parisian lawyer named B. was killed in the following way: He was forced to run while carrying a 100-pound sack of cement, to return to get another sack, and then to make his way back again. He could not hold out for more than an hour; so he was left in peace for the rest of the day. On the following day, however, the SS officer who guarded the squad in the morning tore the lawyer's glasses off and ordered him to run with a cement sack on his back. Exhausted and confused, the lawyer threw the sack down and said to his comrades: 'I am going, goodbye.' He walked away, stepped over the boundary line, and was shot down on the spot." (50)

"There were people who chose to hurl themselves against an electrified barbed-wire fence and thereby commit suicide." (43)

"In certain squads, the work day lasted 12 hours, from noon until midnight or from midnight until noon. There was never a moment, for any reason whatsoever, that was not committed to work. All the routine of daily life—sleeping, eating, personal hygiene, medical examinations—had to be taken care of in the 9 or 10 hours not claimed by the work details." (108)

"In addition, they used us for all sorts of camp duties: taking food to the SS guards, unloading incoming food deliveries, cleaning and sweeping various parts of the camp. For these jobs they always preferred French workers." (87)

"They were completely worn out by the miserable workday and all the grueling labor. They were all dirty and in a state of appalling despondency." (125)

"After a debilitating day in the quarries, all the internees still had to stand at attention for a two-hour roll call." (113)

"Which could sometimes last from midnight until 7 a.m." (117)

"No relaxation was ever scheduled for the prisoners. It was expressly forbidden for them either to stand or sit in the courtyard between working hours." (113)

"Sometimes, to amuse themselves, the SS guards would have us play a sport that would tire us out more in half an hour than a whole week of work." (23)

"In the barracks there were two reasons why it was impossible to get any rest: the lights that burned continuously, and the commotion of people constantly coming and going." (7)

"17 hours work, 2 hours sleep." (117)

"One of the main reasons for exhaustion was the change of shifts. When we changed, we had to work 24 hours without a break. The supervision by the SS guards was terrible then, for the prisoners fell asleep everywhere and that provided an opportunity to mete out new punishments. This change of shifts took place either every week or every other week." (7)

"One time we were made to wait around from 4 o'clock in the morning until 5 o'clock that evening on the pretext of having our pictures taken, and then we were to be sent to the factory until 6 the next morning. Because we did not get photographed that day, we were assembled again at 6 a.m. and made to wait until 1 o'clock in the afternoon, supposedly to be photographed. Altogether we stood for 33 hours straight." (79)

"No rest on Sunday." (66)

"We had one Sunday a month free when we didn't have to go to work in squads, and this Sunday was ruined because we had to work in the camp where we were beaten." (100)

"Sometimes we spent the whole day at roll call." (33)

"The food was just sufficient to keep you from starving to death but not at all enough to enable you to accomplish any meaningful work." (83)

"We had only half an hour to eat. The soup was served in a barracks with room for 150 people. There were 1,500 of us. We were so packed in that the newcomers failed to eat because they could not grasp what sort of gymnastics were required to obtain the soup and to eat it in such cramped quarters. Since so many people had to enter, eat, and leave in that scant half hour, they had to be processed rapidly, and this processing was accelerated by a 'green' (a common German criminal who wore a green insignia and had complete say over the life and death of the prisoners), who would stand on a barrel, wielding a huge club which he used on those who passed beneath him. He usually managed to get 10 to 15 victims." (207)

"Sometimes we had only 15 minutes for the soup, and usually we had to bow down to get it." (103)

"There were days when people would work all day long without rest or food. They would then return at four in the afternoon to the camp they had left that morning at three." (125)

"With such rations, the ability of a normal person to work lasted an average of six months. People who were not strong might last no more than two months. First, they used up their fat, then their muscles, and they would lose 30 to 35 percent of their weight." (93)

"It is only natural that many of them collapsed from total exhaustion. For these unfortunate ones it meant the end was near." (96)

"As many as 50 deportees might go to work in the morning under the supervision of a Kapo. There would also be 50 rations allotted. If the Kapo brought back only 40 or 45 deportees in the evening, the leftover rations belonged to him." (89)

"By the same token, if a guard brought back 15 dead, he got 15 days of vacation." (103)

"One day I heard the following conversation between two Germans, a Kapo and an SS guard:

'How many today?' asked the guard.

'Five,' answered the Kapo.

'That's not very many,' said the guard.

'I'll try to make it ten tomorrow,' said the Kapo. It had to do with the killing of prisoners." (86)

"I saw a Kapo hold the head of a deportee under water until he died." (89)

"I saw how an American of Italian ancestry, called C. L., born in August 1901 in New York, was abused and killed. He had frostbitten feet and was forced to work in spite of his condition. They bound his feet with paper and sent him back to work in the snow. He held out for 12 days before he died." (17)

"Some prisoners had the dangerous job of loading unslaked lime into a wagon. Since they had no shovels, they were forced to handle the lime with their hands. One windy day a young Israeli got lime dust in his eyes and complained to the SS guard, who took him aside and shot him." (39)

"Each person who died meant a 60 mark bonus provided that it happened during an escape attempt. For that reason the SS guards would take the headgear from one of the prisoners and toss it between two rows of barbed wire 10 yards apart, in a region that was considered an escape zone. Then they would order the owner of the headgear to go get it, and if the man obeyed and went into this zone, the guard in the watchtower would shoot him. If the man couldn't decide whether he wanted to retrieve his hat or not, the SS guard would sic the dogs on him, and they would literally tear him to pieces.

"The perimeters of the guarded area were changed frequently in order to make it easy for the prisoners to find themselves on the wrong side of the line without knowing it and be shot." (86)

"The prisoners were surrounded by SS guards who had the right to hit them, to let dogs loose on them that would bite them viciously, and to shoot them for any alleged attempt to escape. The SS guards of the camp exercised this right in brutal ways." (65)

"The foremen, common criminals themselves who had been hand picked, assisted in the torture of the internees as a way of pleasing the camp executioners and of enjoying certain prerogatives." (121)

"The work was overseen by a Kapo. He was responsible for the output of the prisoners and used beatings, whenever necessary, to make sure the work got done. He knew that if the workers' performance was not acceptable, he would himself receive 25 lashes; therefore, he had to prove that he had beaten the prisoners by pointing to the bruises on their bodies." (115)

"While we worked, we were continuously being beaten, either by the foremen or by the Kapos." (87)

"We were treated with extraordinary brutality. They beat us for no reason." (7)

"No matter whether you were a good worker or a bad worker, you got beaten anyway." (98)

"Once I saw two SS officers coming toward me in the tunnel. One of them swore at me and hit me in the face with his fist. I fell on the cement floor and lost consciousness. When I came to, he had disappeared. I never did find out why I had been hit." (31)

"The junior director of the mine used to visit the mines twice a week. He would sneak up on us and for no reason at all use his steel-tipped cane to hit us, one after the other, saying as he did that he was hitting us because we were Jews and that the Jews were responsible for the war. He said: 'We will kill all of you dogs.' Although the Poles who

worked with us were not allowed to talk to us, they told us anyway
that before our arrival they were the ones who got beaten, and that
they were very happy to be replaced by the Jews." (33)

"We were warned that the Block leader was crazy and that we had
to be careful in his presence. He would walk around carrying an enormous whip made of telephone wire nearly half an inch thick and use it
on anybody he pleased." (7)

"From the vantage point of my work station, I noticed that many of
the French prisoners who were put to work gathering and stacking wood
appeared to be disabled. SS junior officers would walk up to them and
start beating them until they collapsed. Then when they were lying on
the ground, the SS officers would kick them in the stomach." (47)

"While the work was going on, the Kapo of Squad 'Petersen,' who
was dissatisfied with the results of the work, ordered an internee to
crawl on all fours while he hit him in the lower back with a heavy
stake. The poor internee was taken to the hospital with three broken
vertebrae and died within 48 hours." (86)

"Every day we had to go out into the fields to dig for potatoes. Ten
hours work, on your knees. If a prisoner sat down on the ground or stood
up, he would immediately be hit with an iron club. If he was not
killed outright, he would most certainly sustain at least a broken arm
or leg or a few ribs." (51)

"I can't tell you how many fractured ribs and split skulls I saw." (12)

"Work in the squad was always accompanied by kicks, punches, and
blows inflicted by a rubber truncheon or billy club or the handle of a
shovel." (87)

"With certain jobs the beating never ceased. For example, those
prisoners who had to push wagons were struck by the SS guards every
time they went past them. It was the same with the field workers who
were constantly beaten by the SS guards. The prisoners assigned to
these squads had no hope of ever coming back." (73)

"The SS overseers constantly reminded the prisoners that they
would not get out alive. The prisoners lived in an atmosphere of
perpetual dehumanization and fear. There, as in all the camps, many
prisoners died from the consequences of repeated, senseless beatings."
(108)

"Work always had to be done in double time." (43)

"Prisoners were absolutely forbidden to move in anything but double
time." (93)

"We were not allowed to stand still for even a few seconds." (87)

"You always had to be in motion." (113)

"You had to run with a load that was unbearably heavy, considering
the weakened state of the people. If somebody collapsed, the SS
guards would use their boots to finish them off. If you had a friend in

front of you who collapsed, you had to step over him, or it meant your death." (43)

"If a person inadvertently slowed down and was taken by surprise, he would be punished. This punishment could take the form of anything from a few lashes with a whip to a long, grueling gymnastics session. Each poor performance was punished with a thrashing, usually 25 lashes on the buttocks. The victim, whose pants had been removed, would be held by two prisoners chosen by the SS guards, and ordered to count out loud as as he received the lashes." (7)

"Those identified as Jews were singled out for particularly cruel abuse." (75)

"No matter what physical condition he was in, a Jew could not survive more than two weeks. For example, a Jew who was so efficient that he could do his work twice as fast (say, pushing a heavily laden wheelbarrow) would obviously not be able to keep up this pace. When at last he showed signs of slackening, he was sure to be struck dead by a blow from a shovel or a pickaxe." (104)

"Work in the stone quarries was real chain-gang labor." (121)

"At that time all Jews had to work in a field unit, climbing up and down the slope of a gravel pit in double time. Up above, SS guards and Kapos supervised their work and monitored the pace of their performance. If they thought that one of workers was 'dragging his feet,' they would wait until he was climbing upward and then simply give him a push and watch him slide with his loaded wheelbarrow all the way back down the slope. For the guards this was a favorite way of passing the time." (104)

"In the quarries there were almost no tools. The unfortunate workers had to transport huge stones on their backs. The exhausted internees had to do their work going up and down a staircase consisting of 108 steps that had been carved into the rocks of the quarry. As their strength gave out, they would very often stumble under their burdens, collapse, and end up crushed at the bottom of the pit. This happened when stones were being transported, some of which could weigh a couple hundred pounds. Four to six internees carried these on their backs and the least false step on the part of any of them and all was lost. This sort of accident, if one could call it that, occurred daily. I saw it happen twice myself." (121)

"In one shipment there were two of these unfortunate Jews, one of whom was a fourth-year medical student. These two friends were put together with the 20 Jews who were already there. They had to sleep under the bed where they were kicked and beaten with a bullwhip. They were assigned to a special squad of 'camp builders' who were involved in the construction of a clinic. The leader of this squad was a common criminal known by the name 'Jim the Frightful.' He is to thank personally for the death of all the Jews who were brought to the camp up until July 1943, at which time he went into the SS.

"One after the other, the Jewish internees were notified eight days before of the date of their death. If, in the meantime, the beatings were too severe, they would be suspended for a few days so that the victims would not die before their time. C. died, if I remember correctly, toward the end of June 1943.

"R., who had greater resistance and a marvelous inner strength, held out until the end of July, beginning of August. I visited him one evening after returning from work. Two days before his death he told me that the Kapos had told him that he was to be killed the day after tomorrow. The last two days became for him a true martyrdom. He refused to walk alone to the line beyond which one was shot. He was led there by the Kapo, and the guard fired the gun. The second bullet killed him. I saw myself how they treated his body. The camp registry bore the citation: 'Shot trying to escape.'

"Others were killed in the following way: They were forced to carry 200 pound stones down into a hole and then carry them back up a ladder, and after a day or two of such work they were given a rope to hang themselves with. If the prisoners refused to hang themselves, the Kapo would gladly give them a hand." (75)

"Almost every week there were executions for various reasons, from stealing a liter of soup to so-called sabotage. (Sabotage was impossible in the tunnel; every screw was inspected twice by Luftwaffe specialists.)

"There were numerous hangings, but what impressed us most by its gruesomeness was the simultaneous hanging of 32 prisoners, accused of sabotage, by means of an electric hoisting device. We were made to stand there and watch. The Kapos and the foremen would hit us if we stopped watching. The condemned went to their deaths with wooden gags in their mouths. The next day 56 more prisoners were hanged for reasons unknown to us." (91)

"I worked 14 months in a weapons factory during which time an act of sabotage occurred in the making of explosives. The Poles who worked there were hanged." (94)

"If you were exhausted some day because of overwork and the SS guard for some reason was not satisfied, you would be sent that evening to the gallows, then to the ovens." (51)

"In the evening we had to march back. If a man was dying, he still had to march. It was in this way that the brother of the publisher of an American newspaper died. We carried the dead comrades home. Each corpse was carried by four prisoners." (86)

"During my time in the quarry—i.e., until June 1944—not a day passed that the prisoners did not return to the camp carrying the dead, who numbered anywhere from 2 to 10." (75)

"Because of abuse by either the SS guards or the Kapos, the internees often died of their injuries." (60)

"200 internees would leave for work and only 120 would return. If there were 150 of them in the evening, that was 30 too many. The Kapo ordered an internee to pick a number. If, for example, the number was 10, then, as the SS guard counted them off, every tenth man had to step forward. For each this meant death." (43)

"The director of a squad that was building an underground factory boasted he could kill off his workers in less than six weeks. Lack of sleep and food, enervating work, everything happening in double time. Those who fell behind were butchered on the spot. The few survivors were taken back to the so-called 'extermination block' of the camp where they died of exhaustion." (109)

"Inmates died like flies. They were piled up like sacks and waited a day or two until a special team with wheelbarrows came from outside to collect them." (7)

"The death rate was so high that in our group of 200 men, 30 to 35 died daily. Quite a few of them owed their death entirely to the beatings that the foremen and the Kapos administered for no reason whatsoever. The ensuing gaps in our own ranks were filled daily with other prisoners." (96)

"The highest death rate occurred among the squads that worked outside the camp. On January 2, 1945, Squad S III contained 3,000 men. On February 22, we learned that 1,500 sick deportees from this camp had been sent back to rest up. By the time they arrived at the train station, 200 of them were already dead. Between the station and the camp, another 160 died. At the end there were only 50 men left. In another squad, out of 4,000 Jews there were 3,600 dead." (84)

"Out of 1,800 prisoners, 600 died in 6 weeks. Elsewhere, in the course of three weeks, only 280 out of 1,800 remained alive." (117)

"Within 2 or 3 months the percentage of dead was between 70 and 80 percent." (63)

"The Jews accounted for 80 percent of the dead in the camp." (84)

"In reality, we were all sentenced to death. Only the interest the Germans had in our work gave us a stay of execution. All of us awaited the day when we would die of total exhaustion or suffocation in a boxcar or gas chamber or by some other means of extermination." (31)

WOMEN AT WORK

"It was a regular slave market. If the manager of a factory, for example, needed 500 women, he would come to the camp and announce that he needed 500 women by a certain date. The whole Block would then be assembled immediately and we would line up in rows of five." (12)

"One after the other we had to file past a review board whose director acted like some kind of slave trader. He examined our eyes, our hands, even the way we walked, and then handed us a mysterious little piece of paper with the letters 'K.W.' and a number on it. This little piece of paper contained our work assignment." (45)

"In addition to the various kinds of camp labor they had to perform, women also staffed the offices." (28)

"Work that was too hard for the men was not unusual for the women. They laid rails, pushed small trucks, pulled rollers." (72)

"They were pipe layers and roofers; they repaired the laundry facilities." (28)

"They chopped wood, felled trees, unloaded ships, built roads, drained swamps, pulled rollers. I myself, together with 19 comrades, pulled a roller." (41)

"Many women were put to work mixing cement, or unloading sacks of concrete from freight cars, or shoveling coal." (125)

"In Hanover we worked for 'Continental,' in the department that made gas masks." (48)

"There were also weaving and sewing studios in the camp for making military uniforms and uniforms for prisoners and also for mending used uniforms, for the dead were stripped and their clothes recycled." (53)

"A lot of women were put to work ripping apart the uniforms of fallen German soldiers. They would have to work on these soiled items of clothing and then eat their soup with dirty hands." (109)

"Our plant made the left wings for Messerschmidts." (12)

"Many women worked in the Siemens factory (electrical appliances)." (67)

"My job consisted of drilling 8-millimeter holes in steel or aluminum with a 15-pound steam hammer. I had to hold this steam hammer in my hands the whole workday, which was 12 hours long." (12)

"All the women who did men's work, as well as those who did women's work—like, for example, weaving—were pushed so hard to work at peak performance that they were not allowed to raise their heads from their work for even one second." (41)

"It was assembly-line work, the pace of which was being constantly accelerated. If at the beginning the conveyor belt came full circle every three hours, at the end it was coming around every 40 minutes, which of course did not give us one free moment." (12)

"To speed up production, the Germans used the following ploys: They promised prizes consisting either of money or Red Cross packages, both of which had been stolen from other internees in the first place. If a woman who was especially adept or had a special talent at her particular job achieved a higher level of production, she would get the prize. But the SS would then demand the same level of performance from all the other internees, arguing that if one person could do it, then there was no reason why the others could not do it, too." (95)

"The few French women who were offered such prizes refused them categorically. It was very noble of them when you realize that the prize consisted of food, which, while it might be of doubtful quality, was of tremendous importance in a camp where people were dying every day of starvation.

"In spite of everything, our production at one point dropped to almost nothing. Nevertheless, we were compelled to act as if we were working anyway or be shoved under a spigot of cold water.

"I am proud to say that the women I was with, all of us French political prisoners, were looked upon by our enemies as the worst possible workers." (120)

"The working conditions were terrible." (45)

"Twelve hours a day or 12 hours a night." (67)

"For 12 hours you were bent over a machine at hard labor." (120)

"Many women worked 14 hours a day; they got up at four in the morning and finished up toward six in the evening." (125)

"We ourselves had to work from eight in the morning until one the next morning." (12)

"When our group had the night shift, we got no more than three hours of sleep during the day. When we got back to camp, the overseer would find still more work for us to do: unloading potatoes, cabbages, and coal. There was always something to be unloaded." (48)

"A certain kind of truck was specially made to be pulled by women. Thirty of us were harnessed to it, and that was the way we transported coal." (85)

"And we still had to march off to work at night." (48)

"In the factory I was not allowed to sit down." (12)

"In August 1944, a sick comrade of ours named G. L. asked to be relieved from braiding rushes, a job which required her to stand all the time, and to be allowed instead to braid corn silk, which could be done sitting down. The overseer refused. A week later our sick comrade died." (51)

"During the first few months, I belonged to one of the teams draining swamps. Sometimes we had to work in icy water up to our knees removing muck." (14)

"Naturally we had to work continuously. Women were sent out in temperatures of 20 to 30 degrees below zero to repair roads or remove snow to make the streets passable. To try to protect ourselves from the cold, we wrapped our feet in rags and paper." (28)

"We were routinely searched to see that we weren't hiding anything." (12)

"It was absolutely forbidden to put even the smallest piece of paper under your clothes to make yourself a little warmer or at least to feel a little less cold." (28)

"While I was very sick, my co-workers asked if the last machine, the one standing right next to the foreman, could be moved back so that I wouldn't feel a draught on my back from the open window; but in spite of their urging, the foreman refused this gesture of humanity, saying: 'It doesn't matter if she dies.'" (2)

"These poor women cried from hunger and thirst." (125)

"But they suffered most from thirst, if they weren't sick from something else. In the evening when I brought a bottle of water for my friends, I had to climb over howling women on the way. I knew how much a single drop of water would mean to them, but unfortunately I had to think first of the eight friends I had originally come there with." (10)

"During work we could use the toilet only at specified times. This restriction was particularly agonizing for us because we all had diarrhea.

"Our new work was taught to us by German civilian workers. Some weren't so bad, but most beat the women and denounced them to the Kommandant when the work was not flawlessly done, which resulted in more beatings and sometimes in a transfer to a disciplinary camp.

"The work was performed under the supervision of officers and overseers who abused us if we took a break or tried to hide from the Germans and who beat us and reported every possible disciplinary violation, particularly our gathering weeds and leaves to supplement our meager diets." (12)

"We were beaten for absolutely no reason whatsoever simply because the SS figured that the pressure to perform was not great enough. Whether you worked or not, it didn't matter. They beat you anyway.

"If a woman raised her head or slowed down on the job, an SS guard would hit her. One of them killed many of our comrades by knocking them down, hitting them with a wrench, and then kicking them to death." (41)

"Once I fell down three times because I couldn't go on. The SS guards used a whip to make us get up." (85)

"In every workshop one or two SS guards, wielding clubs, supervised

the workers and often beat them to death at the least sign of fatigue."
(45)

"We were also supervised by SS matrons who beat us for trivial
reasons. Some were particularly despicable. We gave them the
following names: panther, predator, pug dog, chink, and fat cow." (48)

"When any of our comrades happened to use the toilet without
permission, they were savagely beaten when they got back." (95)

"I saw one worker whose forehead had been split open by an SS
matron who had hurled her against a sewing machine merely because
she spoke." (81)

"I saw SS matrons beat female prisoners to death with a whip." (82)

"The internees were not only constantly beaten by the SS guards but
were also bitten by dogs." (72)

"The SS, who hit us with rifle butts and bullwhips, often sicced the
dogs on us."

"These dogs were vicious; they were ravenous and bit with all their
might." (14)

"The women were so terribly afraid of them that they were sick
with fear the whole day long." (95)

"The dogs were also turned loose in the sleeping quarters to make
sure that we got up." (41)

Chapter 7

Sanitary Conditions

ILLNESSES

"Sickness broke out in the camp. During March and April there were many cases of typhus. Many died. I don't know the exact number because the dead were hidden until nightfall at which time they were buried in the woods behind the camp.

"Some of the diseases included in the epidemic were typhus with skin rash (spread by lice), pneumonia, erysipelas, scarlet fever, and, worst of all, tuberculosis.

"Very often the disease would run its course so swiftly that the patients died within three to four weeks. Not counting the cases of dysentery, 40 percent of the autopsies showed that the patient had died of tuberculosis.

> *Lung Diseases.* Extremely common. 40 percent died from pneumonia alone. (1,950 Danes in something like 60 days.) I treated 41 cases of pneumonia. The pneumonia was particularly bad, while the pleurisy proved fatal in three out of four cases.
>
> *Dysentery.* Two epidemics, the first mild, the second severe (50 to 60 percent fatalities).
>
> *Diarrhea and Enteritis.* Very often they accompanied other diseases and hastened the death of the afflicted persons.
>
> *Abscessed Wounds.* Very frequent.

"In April 1945 there were approximately 2,400 beds occupied in the hospitals and annexes. In addition, there were more than 2,500 patients in dire need of surgery or medical attention. Many of the acutely or chronically ill were not hospitalized.

"In other words, at least 10,000 beds would have been necessary at the beginning of April 1945. More accurate is the number of dead I recorded for the first quarter of 1945. The average monthly number amounted to well over 4,000. The death toll for each month was as follows: 2,000 in January, 5,400 in February, 5,623 in March; i.e., more than 13,000 in three months." (80)

"Almost all of the prisoners died of diarrhea or its consequences or as a result of their dreadfully weakened physical condition." (90)

"By the thousands they succumbed after a while to that most fatal of illnesses: tuberculosis. In my group alone, there were many victims." (103)

"Many young female prisoners died very quickly of tuberculosis. Usually the sick and those whose performance was not satisfactory were sent back to the camp, and I learned of the deaths of most of them in the days that followed." (12)

"Other illnesses cropped up such as malaria, which was allegedly carried by the Greeks. To try to stem this epidemic, they simply sent all the Greek women in the Block to the gas chamber with the excuse that they were carriers of the disease. Soon thereafter all malaria victims were ruthlessly gassed, and I escaped this measure only by a miracle. I had malaria, but when they were drawing blood, they took blood twice from my neighbor. I was, therefore, saved and evaded the gas chamber." (10)

"Countless female deportees who had been out working on the earthworks, particularly the ditches being built to retard the advancing allied armies, came back with completely frozen limbs or with gangrene. On orders of the German nurses, we were told to stick them in one corner of the room and not bother ourselves about them. They could not be operated on. They were mostly Hungarian Jewish women and they all died." (32)

"I had to bandage horrible wounds caused mainly by beatings. The immune system was too weak to resist infection, and the sores and abscesses were difficult to care for, especially in the case of the Jews. The sores were hideous to look at; the streptococci and staphylococci ate away at the muscles and even the bones. The muscles melted into a form of pus that was nauseating.

"According to what a specialist told me, the composition of the soil on which the camp was built had something to do with the attraction and concentration of strep and staph bacilli. For that reason, many of the newly arrived prisoners did not have time enough to become acclimatized and died of sepsis. An example of this was 1,800 men of the Danish police who had been fed by the Danish Red Cross and had not been forced to do hard labor. They had trouble adjusting, and after three months in the camp, all but 56 had died of blood poisoning.

"Many prisoners suffered from hemorrhoids, the result of lying for hours on wooden floors or cold earth while being transported to the camps. There was a high percentage of tumors, caused mainly by lack of nourishment." (90)

"Sickness increased as a result of poor nutrition and unbearable living conditions. Severe stomach disorders and an apparently incurable foot disease spread throughout the camp. The victims' feet would become so swollen that it was impossible for them to walk." (104)

"There were many cases of inflammation of the trachea and the lungs, of dysentery, and of dilation of the cardiac muscles, all of which led to debilitation and almost certain death." (71)

"I could diagnose many sickness from the corpses. In about 70 percent of the bodies examined, pleurisy had taken hold as a result of inflammation of the pleura and the thorax. The hearts of almost as many bodies showed signs of pericarditis.

"80 to 90 percent of the bodies exhibited atrophy of the heart muscles as a result of poor nutrition and extremely low blood pressure. Many of them also showed signs of deterioration of the kidney membrane and other organs brought on by inflammation and hemorrhaging. All of this was the direct result of beatings by SS guards who, having a predilection for those parts of the body, administered their blows especially to the area of the lumbar region.

"The stomach of one corpse was particularly characteristic. It was grossly protracted, its lining smooth as glass as a result of watered-down food." (90)

"The average life span of a prisoner was about six months." (80)

"A French Jew from Yon told me that he had come with a shipment of some 5,000 Jews from France and that only 5 of them were left; most died of typhus. Another Polish Jew told me that from one shipment of 5,000 Jews, only 200 were left." (125)

MEDICAL EXAMINATIONS

"We regularly had to undergo very unpleasant medical examinations. We were made to strip naked in in the courtyard in all kinds of weather." (24)

"These examinations were purely a formality, since the doctor examined five prisoners a minute. You would pass before him naked with outstretched hands, and the doctor would look at you between his fingers and say, 'Good.' We were asked about our occupations. I said, 'university professor' and was designated 'movable.' I also mentioned that I had had polio. On my card this was simply noted as 'childhood illness.' On the basis of this examination many of my countrymen were taken away." (54)

"As part of the routine arrival examination, we had to undress in a hallway. We appeared naked before the doctor and had to spread our legs and raise our arms high; that was it. Even if you told him that you were sick, it didn't matter." (61)

"We women had to appear naked at four in the morning in the courtyard and submit to an examination by two Germans who passed themselves off as doctors. They inspected the soles of our feet, our hands, and our teeth. Later they extracted something from our vaginas, a procedure for which we did not have to undress. There was a young girl among us, a virgin, who was deflowered in this manner." (12)

"One of the examinations took place in February. We waited outdoors by the thousands. Finally, we filed past a German major who was sitting on a table and mockingly sizing us up." (28)

"Those who were sick and did not stop immediately in front of him or who were not fast enough in taking off their pants were hit in the pit of the stomach." (35)

"One night, weakened by hunger and cold, I suddenly got a severe attack of leg cramps. I was taken to the hospital where the head physician accused me of malingering. He tried to force me to stand up, but I was not up to it, so he hosed me down for half an hour with water that was not only icy but suffocating because he sprayed it directly into my face and mouth." (87)

"I saw 65-year-old men undressing outside in the rain and waiting 20 to 25 minutes before they could go in for their examination, and then having to put their soaked clothes on again before returning to the Block. It goes without saying that many deaths ensued from such treatment." (63)

HOSPITAL ACCOMMODATIONS

"In principle, the sick did not go to work but remained in the camp where they endured such torture that finally no one declared themselves sick; they simply either didn't or couldn't get up in the morning or could no longer walk." (121)

"The decisions of a French doctor who was known to prescribe rest for a worker were superseded by one of the German medics who would routinely send 200 to 300 men to work who were too weak to do the job." (108)

"Those prisoners who were beaten by the guards or bitten by the dogs were not allowed to receive any first aid or any kind of help.

"When a Jew had an accident, he was given first aid when necessary. But those who were helped went to the gas chamber as soon as they were healed." (35)

"Even the dying could not all be admitted to the rooms designated for the sick in this place that called itself a hospital." (31)

"Often there was no room in the hospital. Then the sick came back to the Block and died there. Two or three people died each day who could not be admitted to the hospital." (80)

"The gathering of the corpses occurred in the following manner: Roll call took place every day in front of the barracks. The internees were ordered to undress the dead and to bring the naked corpses of their comrades with them to roll call. After roll call, a dump truck would drive through the camp and collect the dead, who were then transported to the crematory." (106)

SICKROOM CONDITIONS

"The infirmary: the building to which the dying were sent to die." (106)

"It was a herding together under terrible conditions. The ward I worked in from December 25, 1944, until April 1945 had 44 beds. We had as many as 152 patients. Most of these patients had tumors, running sores, or diarrhea.

"I saw one patient with a tumor on his leg that had been repeatedly kicked. In one night these injuries brought about the gangrene from which he died. A shortage of medical supplies made it impossible to care for those suffering from diarrhea and impossible to keep them clean. All one could do was help them to the toilets, lay them on the floor, and run a lot of water over them. And there was no way of drying them. In an emergency, you could use the blankets, but it was impossible to dry them, which meant that you would have to put them back on the bed soaking wet.

"It turned out that patients were even more abused in the wards than they were anywhere else in the camp. The SS doctors didn't bother themselves about all these details; they simply let things run their course." (75)

"The first night, the prisoner next to me died, and I had to lie next to his body for 36 hours." (57)

"One evening my bedmate died around 11 o'clock, and I had to remain lying next to him under the same blanket until the following morning." (9)

"They took the women with contagious diseases and laid them in the beds of the uninfected." (24)

"My ward contained about 100 patients who were squeezed into this cramped space without mattresses, without towels, and practically without blankets." (78)

"Everything seemed to be calculated to see that the spreading of the infection was accomplished with the greatest possible speed." (57)

"Before our arrival in Compound 13, Gypsies had lived there who had contagious diseases such as scarlet fever, erysipelas, and dysentery. Their sleeping bags were neither disinfected nor changed. One month after our arrival, all 400 of the women interned in this compound were sick, and many began to die. Among the first was a pregnant woman in her eighth month who had traveled under horrible circumstances. She died, as did her child, who had been born in the meantime." (48)

"By order of the camp commander, all prisoners-of-war who came to the sick bay for observation were put exclusively in the barracks inhabited by the patients with virulent tuberculosis." (110)

"People in varying stages of illness lay mixed together on a threadbare straw mat. Some were feverish, others were very sick with diarrhea. Some died, others were taken seriously ill. From time to time someone would carry a body out and deposit it at the entrance to the sick bay. The street crews came and got them." (57)

"The rations for the sick were carefully allotted, but they were intended for only 200 patients per day, while at least 5,000 patients per day needed to be taken care of. Many patients died of hunger." (84)

"As nourishment, the patients received watered down soup and weak tea; that was all." (125)

"We had 150 dead per day and the bodies were sent to the crematory." (117)

"The number of dead was staggering; I think there were 1,500 in November 1944." (31)

"Within 19 months, 8,500 patients died in the camp, at least 1,900 of them French." (31)

"The death rate amounted to about 60 percent per month." (78)

MEDICATIONS

"There were no medications for disinfection, no sterilized instruments or bandages." (86)

"No help from outside was allowed. Every offer of help from the International Red Cross or from the French Red Cross was turned down by the Nazi authorities." (92)

"Remedies were totally lacking, and most of the time the doctors could provide neither an aspirin tablet nor anything else. Countless prisoners died from a lack of sulfa drugs or as a result of the impossibility of receiving a heart stimulant." (64)

"For diphtheria (which I had in September 1944) there was little or no serum. The German SS doctors declared at the time that Germany was the country that produced the most serum in the world, but it was not intended for us.

"It was especially in the sick bay that you could tell you had wound up in an extermination camp, for all around you people were dying of diarrhea and exhaustion. In my ward of 100 patients, 6 to 8 died each day. Absolutely paralyzed people were brought in who were no longer able to speak their names. They'd be given a shot of oil of camphor, but they didn't respond and died almost immediately. They would then be carried away to make room for others who were dying." (75)

"I was confronted with a very bad epidemic of dysentery. We had practically no available medication of any kind with which to combat this epidemic that eventually killed off thousand of victims." (78)

CARE AND HANDLING OF THE SICK

"They didn't treat us properly, and although we were housed in the sick bay, we received no medication except for an aspirin tablet." (63)

"I saw a patient next to me die unattended from blows that had caused a wound in her lower back. This woman had gone 40 days without nourishment except for a sip of acorn coffee in the morning." (42)

"Among many others, I particularly remember a former French minister who died as a result of a lack of medical care." (84)

"Everything was arranged on the part of the German doctors to bring about accidents. When Doctor M. attended a consultation, he prodded the prison medical personnel to speed up their work, their surgical dressings, and their auscultations, while he ran around in the sick bay screaming like a madman. He drove the doctors as if he were the Kapo of one of the Blocks." (57)

"On April 10, 3,000 patients of all nationalities arrived at the camp from Lublin. The treatment in the sick bay, the hygiene, and the disciplining (at roll call they had to remain lying in filth) had got so much worse that two months later scarcely a third of them were still alive." (102)

"I personally witnessed scenes of sickening brutality in the convalescent compound. Those who were recovering from an operation or an illness and were too weak to work were put in Compounds 38 and 39 and isolated from the rest of the camp. They were abused by the leader of their compound, beaten, and thrown out of bed, deprived of food, and subjected to incessant roll calls." (19)

"One morning one of our comrades had a fever and could not get up. He was lying in the third tier of the bunks, more than six feet high, when the barracks orderly climbed up and threw him down on the floor." (59)

"A 54-year-old prisoner was forced, in spite of the weather and with a fever of 104, to sing and to walk; he died on August 7, 1944." (4)

"One of my comrades from Rouen had contracted a common edema and heart ailment as a result of which his health appeared to be ruined. The overseer S. ordered him one morning to empty his chamber pot even though he by no means had the strength to do it. The poor wretch had to kneel down, in spite of his condition, and try to do as he was told. When he got to the door of his cell, he fell and broke the pot whereupon the overseer immediately flew into a rage and struck out wildly, knocking him back into the cell. Two hours later my friend was dead.

"I was actually a witness to the following event: Another comrade, gassed in the 1914 war and suffering from tuberculosis, found himself for about a year in miserably poor health; he was spitting blood and had withered away to a skeleton. In the shower he trembled when he stood under the cold water. Guard D., a German of French ancestry, doused him with a bucket of icy water, with no regard whatsoever for his condition. His illness got worse immediately and he died shortly thereafter.

"Guards S. and E. repeatedly conspired to punish inmates by methodically throwing them into jail in order to accelerate their debilitation. Many died as a result of this kind of treatment." (52)

"A German who no longer had the strength to clean himself or control his bowels was dragged outside, stripped naked in 10-degree weather, and cleansed with a broom and a bucket of icy water. He died the next day of a hemorrhage." (83)

"One comrade who had sustained a fracture was brought to the hospital where he was first given a cold shower; then he underwent an operation on the fracture without an anesthetic. He suffered very much and had to remain for five weeks in the hospital during which time he received almost nothing to eat. After his release from the hospital, he was assigned to a squad of crate haulers. When the fracture recurred, he asked the SS guard if he could give him somewhat lighter work. With his bullwhip the guard struck him in the face, especially in the mouth, causing his teeth to come loose. Afterwards he was taken to the sick bay where the camp dentist pulled his teeth and split the gold with the SS guard." (39)

"One evening I saw 18 patients being brought back on the shoulders of their comrades. Two SS guards put them in the recovery room, an unheated room with windows left open for 'ventilation' even though the temperature was below zero. They remained without assistance because the guards went to the movies. Eleven died during the night and five the next day; only two remained alive." (17)

"An SS guard named M. was in charge of the camp medical services and a real monster. To work up an appetite for breakfast he would single-handedly strangle two or three patients." (94)

"Even outdoors the sick could find no rest because the 'torture boys' forced them to run around in circles. Those who could no longer stand on their feet or be budged from where they fell were overwhelmed with blows from truncheons and clubs or sadistically beaten with canes." (121)

"One evening the guards had the 'so-called sick' (about 400) come outside. In bitter cold weather they were stripped and taken to the showers where they received alternating hot and cold showers that ended with an icy shower that lasted 20 minutes. Then they were left outdoors naked for an hour. The operation was repeated the whole night through. In the morning only 40 prisoners were still alive. These were beaten to death with axe handles." (39)

"In their diabolical sadism the young SS 'torture boys' of the camp were constantly devising new atrocities. For months they amused themselves by using the heads of patients for target practice. Countless patients were killed in this way." (38)

"60 to 70 deportees or more died in the sick bay. Before they had even drawn their last breath, many of them were stripped naked and thrown out into the snow. One of them called out for two hours for his mother." (39)

"On December 5, 1943, a group of 80 patients arrived from another camp. On the orders of the German doctor, all of them were stripped and forced to spend the night out in the open. The orderly was then ordered to pour buckets of cold water on them. After this night the majority of these prisoners died." (86)

"The infirmary was a place from which you never saw anyone come back alive." (45)

INOCULATIONS

"One day in March, 1945, the Kommandant asked the head doctor the following question:
'How many deaths do you have per day?'
'30,' said the doctor.
'That is not enough,' the Kommandant replied. 'I need 150.'" (49)

"The sick were no longer acknowledged. Those who came in for a checkup or went on sick call, or those who were already admitted to the sick bay, were not allowed to leave. No one was allowed to come out alive." (47)

"Eight days later we reached 220 deaths per day." (49)

"When we arrived at the camp, the internees had warned us: 'Don't get sick, don't go to the infirmary, don't tell anyone that you are sick.'" (43)

"French prisoners told me that it was very dangerous to go on sick call." (55)

"After several attempts the phenol was injected into the heart." (86)

"One week after I arrived at the camp, the head of the compound, Doctor G., a Pole, but recorded as a 'Reich German,' sent for me and my partner, Doctor K., a Slovakian prisoner, led us into his office where SS Sergeant K. sat at a table, and asked me if I would administer the inoculations. When I agreed, a doctor in a white coat, himself a prisoner whose nationality I don't know, said to me: 'I will show you what you have to do. Here is a 5 cc syringe and a needle used for puncturing the lumbar region. You have to put 5 cc of this fluid in the syringe. Be careful not to spray any of it in your eye, for one drop would be enough to blind you.' They were using phenol.

"He had no sooner said it before he had filled the syringe and ordered two naked prisoners to come forward; they were still wearing their belts and were holding bread in their hands. The doctor then said to me: 'Be sure to take careful aim. You have to place the index finger of your left hand on the nipple and your middle finger on the edge of the breastbone, then probe up and down and from left to right, because in spite of what you think, the heart is on the right side. You must draw some blood first to make sure that you are really in the heart cavity and then inject the fluid.' It was no sooner said than done, and the man who a moment before had been sitting on a chair right there in front of him keeled over dead at his feet." (82)

"Many were killed by injections of phenol in the heart." (35)

"Countless prisoners who were very sick and did not have much longer to live received inoculations in the infirmary that killed them in 10 minutes. Their bodies were then slid down a chute to the ovens. At least 5 men died per day and sometimes 30." (1)

"The SS doctors withheld the medical charts of those considered incurable or afflicted with a deadly disease. That meant that the prisoners in question would be killed with a heart injection in the afternoon or evening." (90)

"The sick prisoners who could no longer work or had swollen legs because of malnutrition were examined by the chief physician during morning consultation and sent in groups to Block 20. There they were told that at the entrance to the infirmary they would either take a shower or be deloused. In truth they were taken to a special room where they were told to sit down on a chair. One medic would take the prisoners by the arm, another would cover their eyes with his hand, and a Pole named P. would inject 4 cc of phenol into their heart. The victims would die in a few seconds. The number of prisoners killed by inoculations like this was estimated at 25,000." (86)

"The Greek Jews with malaria or typhus were ordered to report it. In spite of our repeated warnings, many of them obeyed. All of them died from phenol injected into their heart by a junior officer of the medical corps." (104)

"Countless patients were brought to the infirmary where they were given an inoculation; the next day all were dead." (39)

"Out of 800 patients there were sometimes 100 to 150 deaths in one single night. Sometimes I would see maybe 15 comrades arrive at Block 61, and 3 or 4 days later they would all be dead." (78)

"When the German doctors visited the compound and determined that the patients had typhus with skin rash, they gave them inoculations or used them for experimentation. Naturally we tried to conceal as many cases as we could by inserting the entry 'influenza' on the temperature chart in place of 'typhus with skin rash.'

"In June 1943 a small brick annex was built next to the infirmary of Block 8 and connected to the infirmary by a door. This room served as a storage place for the bodies of those in the infirmary who had been injected with a dose of 10 cc of phenol." (35)

"All the patients were divided into two groups: 'Aryan' and 'Jewish.' These groups were divided into subgroups. The first included those patients who were considered curable and should remain in the hospital. The second consisted of patients who were extremely weak from chronic dysentery and from hunger or injuries and who could be cured only by a long stay in the hospital. The members of this group were condemned to death by phenol injections in the heart. Race also played an important part. An Aryan had to be really seriously ill to be sentenced to death by inoculation, while 80 to 90 percent of the hospitalized Jews were 'taken care of' in this way. Many of them were aware of these methods and asked for permission to be a 'suicide candidate,' since they didn't have the nerve to hurl themselves against the high-voltage wires." (104)

"In the infirmary I witnessed the murder of many 'unpleasant' patients. One with dysentery, for example, fouled his sleeping bag; he got an injection of evipan, a dose of 1 g per 10 cc of water. These intravenous inoculations, injected rapidly, brought about immediate death. There was also sepso, an imitation iodine; an inoculation of 40 cc caused death in 20 minutes. I learned that in Buchenwald some victims had their hearts injected with gasoline and even petroleum." (86)

"To speed up the deaths of the prisoners in Block 7—something I saw with my own eyes in August 1942—over a hundred patients were left lying almost naked in an open field, exposed to the sun. They were also left there overnight, and always without food or water. Their struggle with death lasted two to three days. Among those who were murdered in this way were my uncle and my brother-in-law.

"If for some reason the camp authorities had not already arranged some other form of execution, the head of the compound gave his underlings the order to kill off dozens of patients during the night in one of two ways: either a cane was pressed down on the throat of the prostrate patients while two men jumped up and down on either end, resulting in strangulation; or the patients were asked to bend over and then were beaten on the back of the head. The patients would lose consciousness and then be clubbed to death." (35)

"Prior to the installation of gas chambers, the sick were disposed of systematically by means of an injection of phenol acid into the heart, given by an SS noncommissioned officer, or by mass shootings (mainly for the Russians)." (93)

"To the left walked the healthy, to the right the others who were led to the infirmary where they received an inoculation (for Dachau had no gas chambers); then they went to the ovens." (20)

"If anyone in the compound was found to have dysentery, they were automatically sent to Block 61 where they immediately received, instead of help, an inoculation (which was lethal). This way they liquidated all the sick by means of injections in the heart. They had built a small barracks for the administering of these inoculations. It was dangerous to show any interest in Block 61, for then you looked suspicious and might be sent there never to return. 3,000 prisoners arrived at Block 61 in January, 5,400 in February, and nearly 5,000 in March. With the approach of the Americans, the compound disappeared for fear of a possible investigation." (7)

"I had left behind a friend in Block 61, a German anti-Fascist who spoke fluent French, had lived in France, been arrested by the French police, and had been turned over to the Reich by Pétain. He kept me up to date on what was happening in the compound, which no one was allowed to enter at certain hours, especially at noon and between 3 and 4 o'clock.

"He told me—and I was able to confirm this in the days that followed—that he was certain that people had been killed in this compound with injections in the heart. Most of the victims were part of the regular shipments of prisoners. All those who were suffering from dysentery or were suspected of having typhus were herded into the infamous enclosed courtyard, a place I managed to infiltrate twice.

"As an orthopedic assigned to the sick bay, I visited this friend of mine in Block 61 whenever I could. Twice I was really fearful, for I arrived at the moment when they were 'operating.' I felt especially threatened by a German Kapo by the name of H. who came to my orthopedic office right after my visit and told me never to return to

Block 61, or else. . . .

"Both these times I saw naked prisoners in the courtyard (it was 12:30 p.m.). There were about 50 of them lined up, mostly dysentery patients, their bodies completely covered with excrement.

"My friend told me the manner in which the executions were carried out. The SS Adjutant W. and one other officer would do the selecting. Each prisoner who was able to work would be admitted as a patient and sent to his sleeping quarters. The others, between 80 and 100 each day, would have to undress and then go, one after the other, into a room whose furnishings I have already described. There L., assisted by a Polish nurse named M., would give them injections in the heart.

"My friend told me that the victims collapsed after a few seconds and that two other Poles would drag the bodies into an adjoining room while the next victims were already filing in. So in a matter of minutes a large number of people were 'transferred' from life to death.

"In the evening a special detail of hand-picked Polish orderlies would throw the bodies into a cart and haul them off to the ovens. Identification was superfluous, since all the bodies bore a number painted on with aniline dye.

"Of the sick who were being treated in the compound, those whose illness dragged on were condemned to death." (47)

"Countless prisoners in this condition were put to death by means of so-called 'euthanasia injections.'" (169)

ABORTIONS

"Pregnant women in the second or third month were given a scrape; those in the fourth to the seventh month were given a colpohyster-otomy (a sort of lower cesarean section).

"After this operation the woman would be exhausted and anemic as a result of malnutrition and the trauma of the operation. In roughly 10 days the patients were sent back to the camp where they would spend a few days. After a visit from the doctor, who would declare them unfit to work, they would be sent to the gas chamber." (35)

"The method preferred by the doctors was mechanical abortion. The doctor killed the fetus by means of a stab in the head, then attached a cord to it with a weight hanging from one end. The woman, who was tied to the bed, had only to wait for the emergence of the fetus.

"After the doctor had performed his operation, he would allow his patients to linger in terrible pain. The nurses assured me that the pain lasted anywhere from 2 to 10 hours." (1)

"Pregnant women in the seventh or eighth month were given subcuta-neous injections with a mysterious medicine known to induce premature birth. These injections worked. The fetus, whether it came into the world alive or dead, was eliminated. The goal was to induce premature birth by means of injections without mechanical means." (86)

BIRTHS

"Sometimes they let nature take its course and the child would be born in the infirmary." (123)

"As soon as the children were born, they were taken away from their mothers and wrapped in cloth or paper. Then they were taken to Section 3 and lined up in a box, in rows of three, four, five, or six, like kittens or puppies one wants to do away with. The Red Cross ambulance that picked up the sick from the various camps to take them to be gassed also picked up these newborn babies, who were then tossed in among the sick like so many useless bundles." (57)

"If a baby was born dead, the mother would eventually be returned to the camp where, like all the other inmates, whether or not she got sent to the ovens was a matter of pure chance. If, on the other hand, the baby lived, then the two of them would be sent to the ovens together." (123)

"A difficult problem—and a real crisis of conscience—faced the doctors who happened to be internees themselves. If a child died at birth, the mother escaped death. The question then was: Should a healthy baby be sacrificed to save the mother's life? The fact that this was frequently done to save the mother was a reality that shocked many people. The mothers, however, accepted rather easily the sacrifice of their babies as a way of saving themselves.

"You see, the physical and spiritual agony we suffered and the insidious atmosphere of the camp had irrevocably altered our mental outlook." (57)

STERILIZATION OF THE WOMEN

"Sterilization was performed." (35)

"The women were sterilized. In 1944, sterilization equipment was brought into the women's compounds while the women were outside the camp. The number of sterilized women was very high. Sterilization of the women was effected by means of X-rays." (86)

"I saw comrades who were sterilized, I can give you their names." (82)

"I saw sterilization of Gypsies and Jews." (17)

"Above all they sterilized the Gypsies and the Jews but sometimes also the German prisoners who had been caught committing the crime of fraternizing with the foreign workers." (32)

"Sterilization of the women was performed (after an unsuccessful attempt at cauterization) by an operation. Women and even children were brought to me in my section (Block 9 - Surgery) who were left to lie there with open stomachs that had not been sewn up after the operation. We didn't have any kind of bandaging we could use, and only twice a week were we allowed to make bandages out of tissue paper which, after an hour, was torn and shredded. Their wounds were made worse by coming in contact with soiled and lice-infested blankets, while the straw in the mattresses, not to mention the mattresses themselves, was befouled with the excrement of the diarrhea-stricken patients." (32)

"I personally saw several hundred sterilized women, many of whom died of peritonitis." (26)

"I think they also sterilized children, for they took the female contingent between the ages of 7 and 45. That happened in January 1945. They sterilized them without anesthetic, and the children screamed." (41)

"I took particular care in that I used old washcloths to bandage a little girl of 12 who had been sterilized." (32)

STERILIZATION AND CASTRATION OF THE MEN

"In 1943 and 1944 the Germans selected a number of young men of Jewish origin the moment they arrived at the camp. They were between 13 and 16 years old. On the pretext of learning the skill of bricklaying, they were assembled in Block Number 7 where the bricklaying course was taught. Apparently, these 500 to 600 young people were chosen to be sterilized after they had spent a certain number of months in the camp on a particular diet." (86)

"In Block 21 they castrated the Gypsies." (90)

"Thousands of young Greeks were sterilized by means of an electrical device. If after a few months they were still able to perform sexually, they were castrated." (94)

"The Germans performed widespread sterilization and castration on young internees singled out in the camps at Birkenau and Auschwitz." (86)

"One morning I was recalled to Auschwitz from Birkenau. It was May 19, 1943.

"I was taken to the disinfection area where all my clothes were removed and I was given a new camp uniform. Then I was sent to the infirmary (surgical division) where I was ordered to lie down on a bed.

"The next day I was forcibly placed on the operating table, and they tried to give me an injection in my spine. I resisted and succeeded in breaking the syringe, but they overpowered me, 12 to 1, and gave me the injection. Shortly thereafter I felt paralyzed in my lower limbs. It should be pointed out that the same doctor performed operations of complete castration on hundreds of the internees, mostly young people between 20 and 30 years old." (29)

"M. C. saw and can verify that the Germans amputated the sex organs of countless young Israeli men and boys." (39)

"Many priests were castrated; they unfailingly died as a result because the castrations were performed by nondoctors who had no concept of the principles of surgery." (90)

"What was the purpose of all this sterilization and castration?

"It was probably geopolitical. This probability is based on the following: 25 years after the war (assuming Germany won it), the space now occupied by 80 million Germans would not be sufficient to feed and house an additional 15 to 20 million Germans. The Nazi rulers wanted to expand their 'Lebensraum' at the cost of contiguous countries such as France, Czechoslovakia, Poland, and Ukraine. The populations of these regions would, for 25 to 30 years after the sterilization, supply the necessary laborers and then, without offspring, would disappear. It was in these regions, emptied of their native inhabitants as a result of sterilization, that the Germans planned to accommodate their excess population.

"These young men chosen to be sterilized were 18 to 35 years old, all of them strong and, when possible, without afflictions. Lying on a plank, each of them had to expose his scrotum to the effects of the X-rays. The doctor himself examined them to make sure that the testicles had receded into the scrotum and not into the groin. The treatment with the X-rays lasted five to six minutes. This time lapse had been established after a great many tests.

"After the treatment, the young men, whose number and date of sterilization had been entered in a special register, were returned temporarily to the camp. The clerk in the orderly room received a list with their names and numbers and they were exempted from selection until further notice.

"Either a few weeks or months after sterilization, the young men in Auschwitz, Block 21 (surgery), would be taken into a laboratory where they were questioned about the symptoms of any 'problems' since the sterilization: sexual desire, nocturnal emissions, indigestion, memory loss, depression, etc. . . . Then they were forced to masturbate and to catch a drop of semen on a small plate for microscopic examination. If the physiological prerequisite for masturbation was lacking, then an erection was achieved by massaging the prostate.

"After a few such treatments the Germans found that the massage tired out the masseur, so they found another system by means of a crank which was inserted into the anus of the poor patient. A few turns of the crank were enough to bring about an erection and the discharge of semen. The semen then underwent a bacteriological examination to determine the vitality of the sperm, assuming it lived long enough.

"In 1944, the Germans brought a special microscope to the camp that they called a 'fluorescent microscope' and that operated on the principle that a living cell could phosphorize whereas a dead one could not. That allowed them to separate dead sperm from live." (86)

"Castration was not always complete. Sometimes they amputated the entire scrotum, sometimes a quarter, sometimes a half or a third, according to the instructions and the purposes of the doctors.

"In other cases castration was two-sided; that is, total.

"The testicles, or a fragment thereof, were placed in a tube sterilized with 5 to 10 percent formalin and shipped to an institute in Breslau for the study of tissue.

"I myself was once present at two castrations.

"The incision was made in the groin, a one-sided or two-sided incision depending on whether it was a total or partial castration. They stretched the testicle muscle, extracted the testicles, tied the blood vessels, and proceeded to the removal of parts of the testicles. Then they sewed them up with a few stitches.

"After the operation the young men were placed in Room 5 of Block 21 under the supervision of one of the German orderlies specially trained to care for patients following that sort of procedure.

"After a stay of 8 to 10 days, the patients were placed in Room 1 of Block 21, where I was the attending physician.

"For many, healing took place without suppuration; for others there was suppuration followed by all sorts of complications that lengthened the patients' stay in the surgical wing and put them in danger of being 'selected.'

"In many cases the castrated who had been sterilized by the physical method came to the surgical wing with seemingly normal phlegmonen in the groin. In two cases, careless opening of the phlegmonen resulted in death from sepsis.

"It is reasonable to assume, from the systematic extermination of the Jews in the camp, that sterilization was tried on them with the intention of applying it to non-Germans, non-Jews." (86)

THE GERMAN MEDICAL STAFF

"The internees with medical degrees were not used as doctors but primarily as corpse bearers. Those who actually did function as doctors were SS personnel who usually had had only very limited medical training . . . and we served under their command." (93)

"I was under the command of a German orderly who was a noncommissioned officer. He would arrive at consultations with a stick in his hand and beat the prisoners. One day he asked me if I would mind giving some injections of tecrein in order to kill certain prisoners, because in his opinion there were not enough dead in the camp.

"The medical unit was staffed and run by German prisoners, none of whom had professional credentials or were either doctors or nurses. The head Kapo was a former German convict and the others were carpenters, butchers, and shoemakers. But they were the ones who decided on the admission or rejection of the sick. Take, for example, the case of Professor Richet, who ran a department but who was now being supervised by a former German carpenter. All this occurred with the knowledge of everyone, including the SS, and with the approval of the chief physician of the camp." (78)

"My boss, who 10 years earlier had been a blacksmith, was now head of the department. He simplified his job by using standardized diagnoses that he merely copied out and sent to Berlin. He didn't worry about the rest. He had about eight ready-made pathology reports that he regularly copied and randomly assigned to each corpse." (90)

"Surgical work was handled by a German who professed to having been a Berlin surgeon. He was really just an ordinary prisoner who killed his patients right and left out of sheer incompetence." (17)

"The medical personnel consisted of an Aryan German infirmary director who had been a pipe fitter in civilian life and who performed all the surgery." (87)

"The leadership of the compound was in the hands of two German orderlies, unscrupulous people who, assisted by a bricklayer named H., performed operations on the spot. In fact, H. rather liked to perform major operations anytime, anywhere, and had once amputated a leg that had only a minor infection." (47)

"In late 1943 and early 1944, an operating room was outfitted in which major surgery took place. In order to get some practice, Doctor T. ordered all prisoners with fractures to be operated on. After these operations, he made choices among his patients, declaring most of them unable to work and sending them to the gas chamber.

"Some of the staff doctors in the hospital tried once to hide a few patients. Doctor T. threatened them with death if they ever tried such a thing again. The same Doctor T., in order to get more practice, also ordered women to be operated on for fibroma and all sorts of gynecological growths." (35)

"In Block 21 (the surgical Block), the doctors 'practiced.'

"Every prisoner of Jewish ancestry who complained about stomach troubles was subjected immediately to all the routine examinations: blood tests, examination of the gastric juices, tests for blood in the stool, etc. Independent of the outcome of this examination, it would often be declared that the victims had stomach ulcers and would have to be operated on. After the operation, these people did not receive the care their condition required, not even a milk diet. A few days later these victims died in the gas chamber.

"Doctor K., who received his degree in 1943, wanted to learn various methods of amputation; so instead of making a small incision to remove a tiny growth in a finger, for example, he would cut the the whole finger off. In the case of a growth on the leg, K. performed amputations according to a variety of surgical methods where just a tiny incision would have sufficed. The victims always ended up in the gas chamber anyway.

"Among the recent arrivals in the camp, P. chose those with fractures and operated on them according to the standard methods presented in the German handbooks." (86)

"The room for septic surgery was always entrusted to German internees who had no professional expertise. These people were responsible for the deaths of an incredible number of prisoners as a result of inappropriate surgical operations which were performed on patients simply for the purpose of medical experimentation." (20)

"The chief physician of the camp performed operations at whim and usually without anesthetic (amputations, castrations, ovariectomies, etc.); 8 out of 10 of those operated on died of sepsis." (109)

"We laid a young man on a stretcher who had umbilical hernia, and a young SS doctor, who had never before operated, wanted to practice on him. I took the young man into the operating room and learned from the stretcher bearer who carried him out that he had died that same evening." (90)

"Many German doctors operated conscientiously, but I saw instances, too, where after an ulcer operations, they would bring the patient meat and potatoes. A short time later they would send him to the gas chamber." (35)

Chapter 8

Medical Experiments and Vivisection

"The Germans conducted medical experiments for which they reserved several barracks. The guinea pigs were, of course, the prisoners." (86)

"It is important to understand what I am saying: The guinea pigs were human beings, and destructive materials were tried out on them —a new gas, maybe, or a flammable liquid—as well as cures in the form of vaccinations or antivirus serums." (69)

"In the Neuengamme infirmary they conducted tuberculosis experiments. A doctor came from Berlin once a week. He organized and personally directed the experiments, while two French doctors observed. They often told me about it, but they were extremely discreet, for they feared retaliation, and kept back a lot of details they intended to make known when they got back to France. Unfortunately, I'm afraid both of them perished.

"One of them told me that this experiment was absolutely grotesque, that the method they used was like using a cannon against a mosquito. In other words, the method was extraordinarily brutal and far more dangerous than the illness itself." (73)

"In Block 20 there was a large room full of patients with tuberculosis. The Bayer Company sent medication in ampules without any sort of labels. It was from these ampules that the tuberculosis inoculation was formulated. Never were these victims gassed, but one knew their deaths would occur very shortly. All the tuberculosis patients in the camp formed an infected mass that hastened the progress of a disease already accelerated by deplorable hygienic conditions.

"During autopsies, they removed parts of lungs and tracheas which were sent for study purposes to one of the corporate laboratories.

"150 Jewish women, who had been 'bought' by the Bayer Company from the camp authorities at Auschwitz, were put in a women's compound outside the camp and made to participate in experiments with unidentified hormone preparations.

"A German institute demanded that experiments be made with the anesthetic evipan in the form of intravenous injections. It was, of course, the prisoners at whose expense this experiment was conducted, especially in the camp at Bune. For this purpose, 6,000 ampules of evipan were ordered from the SS infirmary." (86)

"Buchenwald was a large research center for the study of typhus. It was under the control of the SS Hygiene Institute in Berlin, whose director was a leading physician in the SS. This research center, housed in Block 46, was luxuriously furnished and outfitted with up-to-the-minute equipment. It included a diagnostic center, a laboratory, and space for the preparation of vaccine (for the German army). Since it was practically impossible to preserve the typhus bacteria in a culture the way it is done with most other microbes, the typhus culture was preserved in living individuals. Every individual was a living culture of typhus microbes." (93)

"Quite often they tried new vaccines on the prisoners." (69)

"They received vaccines, which they were supposed to try out and improve, from the Weigl Institute in Krakow and from Italy. They were supposed to use healthy, young 'common criminals' (greens) as guinea pigs, but since it was the Kapo who did the choosing, anyone at all in Block 46 could be sent, so even political prisoners and resistance fighters were picked. They sent anybody there they wanted to get rid of.

"Cross-section of the guinea pigs:

1. Many were volunteers because there was good food, decent treatment, and no work. For many it was also the hope of living a few weeks longer.

2. Others were officially selected from among the 'greens' (common German criminals). For a vaccine test, they took, for example, 100 persons. 80 were given a preventive vaccine. 15 days after the last vaccination, the same prisoners would be injected intravenously with 5 cc of the virulent blood of a full-fledged typhus patient in a full-scale crisis. At the same time, the 20 remaining prisoners who had not been vaccinated got the same injection. Within five days these 20 were either dead or dying, for no one had ever been known to survive such an inoculation. Ordinarily, it took only a tenth of a cubic centimeter to cause death.

"Since not all those who had been vaccinated died from it, the Germans drew up evaluation charts of the vaccine showing an effectiveness curve which indicated the speed and number of deaths in relation to those who survived. After two or three months they could predict precisely how many would survive when the vaccine had been administered. These survivors were then 'liquidated' by means of an injection of phenol into the heart." (7)

"In 1944, 200 persons were put at the disposal of Doctor von H., who immunized 150 against exanthematic typhus and used the remaining 50 as guinea pigs. Ultimately all 200 were inoculated with the typhus vaccine. If by the end of the experiment the victims had not died, they were killed and cremated." (115)

"At the end of October 1943, our pathology department received an order to send very good anatomical slides to the most important German universities as quickly as possible. At the same time, special stations were opened for tuberculosis and histology with instructions to study without delay all forms of tuberculosis for the purpose of preparing histological slides. Meanwhile, a whole collection of specimens of healthy organs, including more than 2,000 slides, was to be sent to Innsbruck University. These slides were expensive because the specimens came from absolutely healthy people who were then either hanged or sent to the ovens." (90)

"In Block 20 the Germans were also experimenting with a sulfamide preparation designated B 1034 that was used on a great many patients. This medication appeared to be generally effective except in the treatment of abscesses and wounds. Research into the usefulness of B 1034 was continued in Block 21 (surgery) on a large number of patients, but the preparation still had no effect on wounds and abscesses. Several cases of sepsis resulted in death despite treatment with this medication." (86)

"New toxins and antitoxins were tried out on the prisoners. Of those prisoners who spent time in the building used for 'experiments,' none came out alive." (106)

"One day some German nurses came to the sick bay in Cellblock 10 and asked: 'How many of you have trouble sleeping?' Several young women raised their hands. Eighteen of them were given more or less strong doses of a white powder we didn't recognize but which we took to be morphine. Of the 18, ten were dead by the next morning. It was obviously an experiment.

"In another camp they experimented in all the wards, especially on older women. These women were given a white powder, and the next day there were 60 to 70 corpses.

"In September 1944, I watched them select ten healthy men and give them a medication that had the color and smell of rum. They all went promptly to sleep. In the night four died." (36)

"Polish priests were inoculated with malaria and with pneumonia bacteria. Many of them died. And a German priest was given a double dose of malaria bacteria." (21)

"During my stay, there were other experiments in Cellblock 46 having to do with attempts to find a treatment for burns caused by American phosphorus bombs. A whole series of medications had been tried without success. So they picked out 50 Russians and burned their backs with phosphorus, withholding medication from some of them. They then observed the difference in the time it took for the burns to heal between those who had received medication and those who had not. Three months later, when the experiment was concluded, those who survived were liquidated." (7)

"One Sunday they summoned four convalescents who were in reasonably good shape and had each of them drink a glass containing a sleeping potion whose lethal dosage they wanted to determine. This medication had been shipped by the Bayer Company to Auschwitz 'for experimental purposes.' Two of the guinea pigs were given a sleeping potion mixed with an emetic. All four guinea pigs were then taken to Cellblock 19 where a doctor was following up on the results of the medication. Two of them vomited but survived after 11 hours of sleep. The other two died that same evening.

"The next day the two survivors, along with two new guinea pigs, were used in a second experiment. They were given a new solution to drink. Two vomited and the other two died." (86)

"About this time work was being done on technical preparations for the V 3 rocket, and they needed to test on humans the strength of the poison to be contained in this new weapon. So, one day they got six Kapos from Cellblock 46 and scratched their arms with a poisoned needle. Then they were taken by car to the corpse depository at the crematory, and we who worked in either the crematory or the dissecting rooms were ordered to leave our posts at once and to stay away for at least three hours. When we returned three hours later, we heard agonized screams and were immediately sent away again. The experiment with the new poison was a failure because it did not take effect fast enough. There would still be enough time to take an antidote. Ultimately, the plan was dropped on the grounds that the English might retaliate with something just as deadly. After all, it was said they had at their disposal even more advanced means of chemical warfare than the Germans." (29)

"In Room 15 of Block 28 there were 30 prisoners divided into three groups of 8 to 12. The guinea pigs in the first group were injected with petroleum under the skin of both legs. It was a subcutaneous and very deep injection of 2 to 3 cc of petroleum. Eight days later an abscess appeared; this was lanced and the pus was sent in a sterilized, hermetically sealed vial to an institute in Breslau.

"Other experiments were performed on the second group of ten men who had their skin irritated with various chemical compounds. Many were treated with an 80 percent solution of aluminum acetate. The treatment was administered every day for a week, sometimes on the shoulders, sometimes on the legs, but always on the same spot. Soon thereafter a bad skin irritation appeared, which in many cases led to deeper ulceration. Biopsies were then taken from two levels (one superficial and one deep), placed in sterilized vials, and sent immediately to Breslau for examination. It should be noted that these abscesses were hard to heal. It took one Hungarian prisoner seven months to recover.

"Others, on the other hand, were treated with a black powder on the upper surface of their shoulders.

"At the entrance to Ward 13, the third group was given a small breakfast consisting of 250 grams of white bread and some weak tea. At a predetermined hour K. had them gather in a special room where they were required to take, in his presence, 15 to 20 acridine pills. Then they were sent back to Room 13 and given a container for their urine. Every day they took a urine test, which was then sent by special delivery to Breslau. On the third day, the prisoners who had taken acridine developed jaundice. These urine deliveries went on for three weeks with daily analysis. These experiments continued from August 22 to October 25, 1944.

"Cellblock 10 held 350 to 400 women who served as guinea pigs for experiments being conducted by Professor G. of the Breslau medical faculty. The Germans wanted to try out artificial insemination on a few of the women. Apparently, research and experimentation on previous victims in the camp had remained inconclusive. I believe that the women on whom this experiment was performed have no wish to speak about such a traumatic experience.

"Another group received injections of sex hormones. The ampules containing the medication were delivered by the same professor, who brought them in his briefcase. The injections were given under his supervision. It was impossible to determine the composition of the medication that was injected, let alone the results, since everything was kept so secret. As a result of these injections, many women developed abscesses, which were removed in Cellblock 10.

"In a third group, between 15 and 20 women had surgical operations on their sex organs in Block 10: for example, hysterectomies or injections of a cancer-fighting fluid into the womb of women who had cancer of the womb. This fluid was injected through a catheter equipped with a special filter in order to extract the cancer cells. This was done to test a cancer vaccine that would intercept the virus in the cancer cells passing through the filter.

"A 25-year-old woman from the Auschwitz camp, who was being treated in Cellblock 10, died after the Germans left. The autopsy revealed the presence of cancer of the womb, the result of an inoculation she had received six months earlier. This case is the subject of a report by a Russian investigative commission.

"A fourth group received injections in the uterus with a special preparation sent from a pharmaceutical company. The purpose in doing this was to find something other than lipodol (whose manufacture was very difficult and costly because of a shortage of oil) that could be used in X-raying the ovaries. This medication caused severe pains and its effects still remain uncertain.

"The fifth group of women in Block 10 were under the supervision of Doctor W., assistant to Professor S. from Cologne. The latter operated a photomicroscopic apparatus for color pictures. He would photograph the neck of the uterus of women between 35 and 45. After the photographs were taken, he would remove a piece of obviously healthy uterus and send it to the laboratory of the Breslau Institute for Histo-pathological Research." (86)

"From a doctor, who acted as an expert witness for the state police, I learned of the discovery of 54 histological slides which were found after the Germans evacuated Strasbourg. These plates were discovered in the following way: When the French reoccupied Strasbourg after the Germans had left, they discovered that there had been a scientific organization within the Strasbourg faculty that had been in constant touch with the Struthof concentration camp.

"All the members of this organization, from the presiding doctor to the lowest laboratory assistant, had belonged to SS groups. In one room there were 54 slides which looked at first like something you would throw in the wastebasket. But the doctor's daughter, who had testified for the prosecution, thought that these slides could be of medical interest. They were brought to me in the hope that I could figure out what it was all about, since it was assumed they had something to do with the research at the Struthof camp. The police found out that there had been continuous shipments between the camp and the laboratory. Furthermore, in a refrigerator in the laboratory, bodies were discovered on which operations had been performed. These victims had clearly been killed for the purpose of an autopsy after the experiments were concluded.

"These 54 slides stunned me, for they had something to do with human testicles. After I had studied them more closely, I realized that they had to do with testicles on which someone had conducted experiments by means of injecting some sort of stimulant." (13)

"The doctors were particularly fond of picking out women who were having their period. They callously informed them that they would have to die in four days. They wanted, they said, to observe the effect of this announcement on menstruation." (116)

"A Berlin histology professor had the audacity to disclose, in a German magazine, his observations about the bleeding that women experienced after receiving bad news. This research was done on prisoners with normal periods who had been told that they were to be shot. This caused internal bleeding which this doctor then studied." (13)

"Blood was taken from countless prisoners against their will and used in transfusions for German soldiers. When a prisoner resisted such bloodletting, Doctor S., or his orderly F., would punish the reluctant donor so mercilessly that the poor prisoner would have to be carried out on a stretcher. This treatment was repeated until the prisoner gave in." (52)

"In Birkenau the Germans gathered together a lot of twins of all ages from whom they took blood samples for a Wassermann test in order to study blood groups and determine hereditary weaknesses. The Germans performed a number of operations on the prisoners. For example, they performed, quite arbitrarily, the operation for Leriche's syndrome (an occlusion of the aorta).

"Early in 1942 the Germans began performing experiments by injecting air into the veins. They wanted to find out how much compressed air could be injected into the veins without causing an embolism. I have no precise information about the results of this experiment.

"In the same room intravenous injections with a 33 percent solution of hydrogen superoxide were given, which immediately caused death. There was an attendant difficulty in that when the veins were not visible, the injections frequently missed the mark, and the fluid injected into the tissue would cause unbearable pain and a violent reaction on the part of the subject of the experiment. This method was found to be uncomfortable and unproductive and was given up." (86)

"Hormone tests on pederasts: In the camp were homosexuals, condemned by the German courts, who wore the pink triangle. The experiment consisted of injecting a hormone into their veins in an attempt to rid them of their inclination towards pederasty." (72)

"The Germans likewise experimented with a method of electric shock treatments on the mentally ill. This method consisted of placing paddles on either the temples or the forehead and the neck and letting an electric current pass through. The result of this experiment was catastrophic. There were a great many deaths, and further experiments using this method were discontinued since they were not working out well enough." (86)

"One day the aforementioned university professor from Strasbourg arrived at the camp along with an air force officer. They demanded 30 strong, young internees whom they promptly isolated in a cellblock. Half the cellblock was secured, and no one except the professor, the officer, and me was allowed to enter. I was directed to care for the sick and observe the course of the disease. Even the SS officers were not allowed to enter the cellblock, and all of us were forbidden to report what went on there.

"Here's what I saw: The officer and the professor put on their gas masks. Then they sprayed the palms of the prisoners' hands and the inside of their forearms with about 10 cc of a substance called vogan. Ten prisoners received 15 drops of vogan, ten others eight, and the rest nothing.

"'The sick remained for an hour, their bare arms outstretched, and waited. Then they were put to bed. The first evening the sick began to cry with pain. The inoculation area was covered with a rash. Soon their entire bodies were covered with it. They had inflammation in their eyes and lungs. I did my best to help them. I finally went to bed about midnight, and the next day I had to state that I had seen nothing. An officer showed up, not to aid the sick but to photograph them. From this day forward they were photographed every day, but no one bothered about them although they howled like wounded animals. Soon they became deranged, half crazy. The first patient died in two weeks (on December 21, 1942). His body was sent to Strasbourg. After that no bodies were allowed to leave the camp. The autopsies were performed on the spot. They revealed the following results: retrogression of the brain, lungs filled with pus, cirrhosis of the liver. The survivors were half blind and their lungs were diseased." (115)

"It came to light later that these experiments on people were of absolutely no importance and could have been performed with comparable results on animals; that is, if one assumes that there was anything of true scientific value about them in the first place. The end was just as inhumane as the means." (13)

"Instead of experimenting on guinea pigs, rabbits, and mice, it was easier and more exciting to experiment on people.

"Representatives from the medical profession came from time to time to Berlin to reinforce the personnel performing medical experiments." (106)

"The Germans had a gas chamber built in a specially designated building in order to test an asphyxiating gas on human victims." (65)

"A hermetically sealed shed with windows made it possible to see inside the room. In there an ampule containing 2 to 5 cc of poison gas was broken. The doctors congratulated themselves on the excellent results of their experiments. These doctors also conducted experiments in a gas chamber outside the camp. On August 10, 1943, 86 women were gassed and their bodies immediately cremated.

"It is a matter of record that 15 women were gassed on August 11, 1943, 14 women on August 13, 1943, 30 men on August 17, 1943, and 29 men on

August 19, 1943. Approximately 1,600 women and more than 10,000 men: that is the total number of those victims gassed in the Struthof camp." (115)

"One day all Gypsies and Hungarian nomads were assembled. They were brought to the gas chamber as an experiment. The Germans asked for volunteers. Nobody volunteered, of course, so the Germans pushed the Hungarians in. Half of them died. The exact number of those who died in the gas chamber that day I do not know." (21)

"A German architect drew up the plans for one of these infamous buildings, German scholars came up with the concept and saw it through, and ordinary Germans watched through the peephole as men and women were being murdered in this death camp." (65)

"Block 41 was used for medical experiments and vivisections.

"In one of the specially designed rooms, an operating table equipped with slanted grooves for better blood drainage was used for vivisection operations, which three well-known German professors performed in front of their students.

"The experiments included about 100 victims. The victims were usually Polish Jews. They were sent from Struthof on the orders of the doctors responsible for these experiments and had no contact whatsoever with the other prisoners.

"Twice, patients in groups of 20, whose leg muscles had been exposed, were treated with a medication. After the bandage was removed, a fistula would appear. An SS doctor from Berlin arrived personally to examine it. These victims were chosen arbitrarily from a group of patients who were in convalescence following an operation." (65)

"I knew one of them who lived to talk about his first operation, but not his second. It was clear they killed him to keep him from talking." (80)

"In the archives there is a report of a doctor who complained about the poor health of the people sent to him and requested 90 new victims in good health for projected experiments." (65)

"In Block 17, 200 children were used for sterilization experiments." (117)

"There was a compound at Auschwitz that was especially reserved for medical experiments on women who were chosen from among the healthiest. They had their ovaries, etc., removed without any anesthetic." (103)

"The guinea pigs were Polish women. They were all political prisoners. Many died from the experiments, others were shot; only 60 of them remained alive." (122)

"In the Ravensbrück infirmary, experiments on Polish women definitely did take place. The healthy were selected for experiments with bone transplants. The bones to be transplanted were earmarked for men serving in the army." (41)

"Once they were through taking blood or removing a uterus or a spinal cord, they simply let the victims die." (117)

"Once we saw some Polish women return from the hospital with ugly scars on their legs. Surgeons had come from Berlin especially to perform vivisections on them (grafting of bones and muscles). We heard of similar experiments every day." (45)

"I did some careful investigating of my own into the case of these Polish women whom we called 'guinea pigs.' These women were all condemned to certain death. They were being used for research on gangrene for which the German doctors were seeking a serum; at the same time, extractions from fragments of their bones could be used in other kinds of grafts. These bone fragments were supposed to be used in special research to aid front line soldiers. From these women them-selves, and from observing their hideous muscle injuries, I know that the operations were performed under the following circumstances: The 'patients' were dragged kicking and screaming into the bunker and strapped to the operating table. Nobody even bothered to remove their shoes while their legs were being operated on." (67)

"In Ravensbrück I saw women whom the Germans had used as guinea pigs for their experiments. Some had had their spinal cords removed, some their bone marrow, some their genitals." (120)

"Last year, when the final 'guinea pigs,' who were being rounded up to be operated on, rebelled, they were dragged into the bunker and operated on on the spot. They were anesthetized, but they were not washed, and they were laid in their dirty uniforms on the operating table. After the operation, they remained there for weeks, cared for by one of their own, a woman who, even though she was not a nurse and had no experience whatsoever, did her utmost to take care of them as best she could." (122)

"Once 50 healthy Polish women were selected for an experiment in neurological surgery. I saw them return from this torture with exposed nerves. Many died of it. At the same time the doctors also performed breast amputations." (26)

"Afterwards, those on whom many experiments had been made were sent directly to the gas chamber." (103)

"So that no trace would remain of these operations, the bodies of the victims were carefully burned." (65)

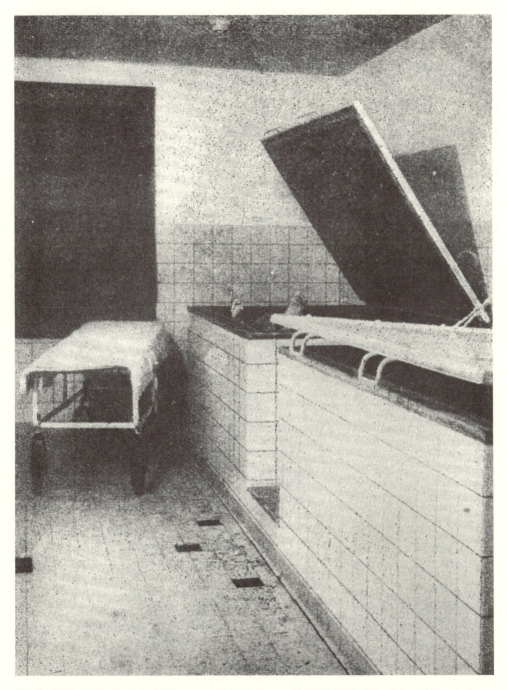

Human "guinea pigs" were often immersed in icy water, sometimes for "medical reasons," sometimes just for "fun"

Jigsaws like this were used for vivisection and for dismembering corpses for medical experiments

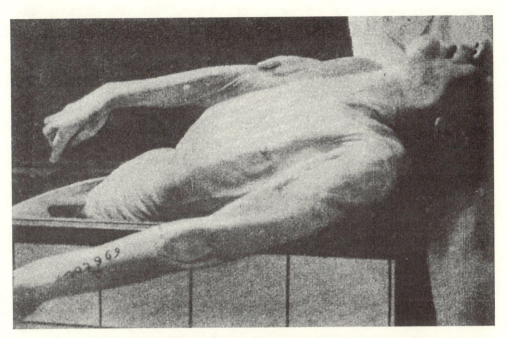

Human cadavers were butchered like farm animals—and for the same purpose (above and below)

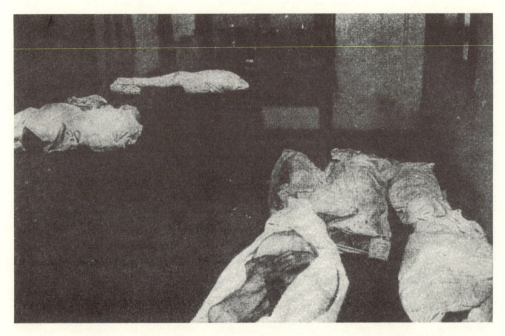

The orderly arrangement of the corpses adds a macabre touch to an already grisly scene
(above and below)

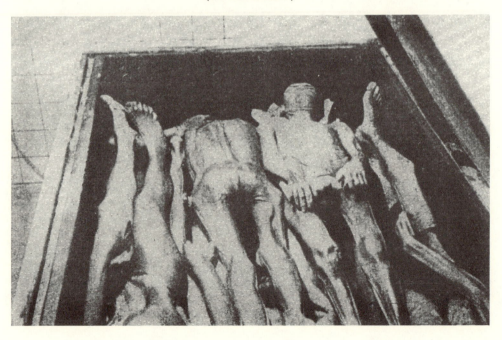

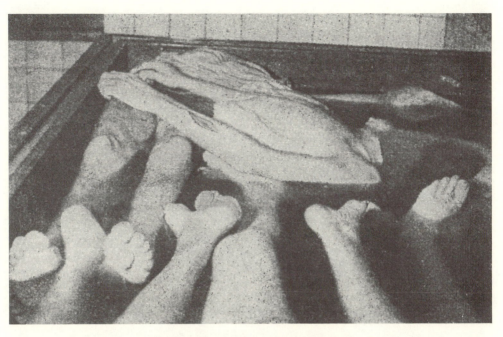

The ultimate indignity (above and below)

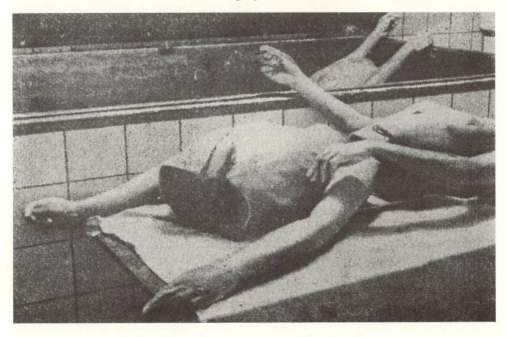

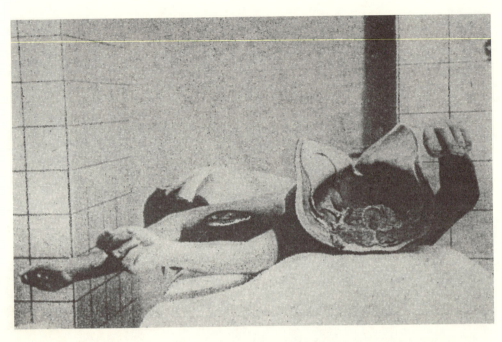

Gross abuse of a corpse does not begin to describe atrocities like these (above and below)

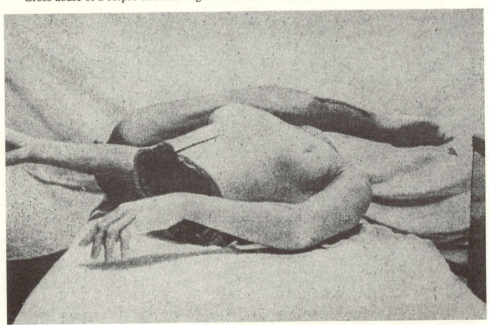

Chapter 9

Various Methods
of Execution

"During 1942 and 1943 there were executions almost every day. These executions took the form of hanging for prisoners from the East and the firing squad for the others (Norwegians, Dutch, Belgians, French). If for any reason a prisoner displeased a guard, the guard would hand him a rope and dare him to hang himself or else be shot in the head in a concrete bunker specially constructed for that purpose." (65)

"According to camp regulations, for every execution, a guard was to receive a bonus consisting of 1 ounce of brandy, 3 cigarettes, and 1 bratwurst." (156)

"On the night of September 1, 1944, 300 internees were chosen at random and executed (shot in the back of the head or hanged), and their bodies were thrown into a cellar where a sea of blood reached a level of ten inches. Since their names were not listed anywhere, we couldn't be sure of the exact number. But we were fairly certain that the group consisted of partisans from the surrounding area." (25)

"Many of those who were condemned to death were taken to the ovens and either hanged first or burned alive. There were anywhere from two to five per day (the inmates who worked in the crematory could attest to this)." (38)

"Those who were crazed or sick were brought to the laundry rooms where they remained two or three days without shoes. The SS guards confiscated their still warm clothes. Then, in nothing but their underclothes, they were hauled off to the ovens." (98)

"At the same time, some unconfined foreign workers from outside who were wearing civilian clothes got mixed in with the inmates and were taken to the ovens after first spending a night in prison waiting to be hanged. The hangings were carried out by inmates at the command of the SS guards who were themselves common criminals." (38)

"There were two notorious incidents involving the execution of French, Canadian, and English paratroopers, the first one in July, the second in October of 1944. The first time there were 11 victims; the second time 17 or 18. Four paratroopers were able to escape death with the help of French and German anti-Fascist political prisoners." (71))

"In August 1940, 1,100 Poles arrived at the camp. On the first day eleven were taken to a quarry and shot. After five months, only 300 of them were still alive." (56)

"Sometimes they'd say: "There are too many Jews here." Overnight 100 men would be killed. An SS guard would take care of that by either strangling them or bashing their heads in." (35)

"I watched as SS guards dragged bodies out of a neighboring barracks. The bodies were naked, and the guards dragged them by the feet and piled them in a heap. I counted more than 80 bodies. The day before, in one of the barracks, the SS guards had carried out one of their routine 'cleaning-up operations' during which they had succeeded in beating to death every person in the barracks with iron clubs." (51)

"One day the Block leader selected ten orderlies (including me) and sent us running to Block 11. When we got to the courtyard of the Block, I was appalled at what I saw. There, like a stack of firewood, was a pile of bodies six feet high. They had been stacked in a certain way so that the blood would drain off into grooves that led away from the building. But the blood couldn't drain off entirely and had formed a pool that was ankle deep.

"Another day a big van drove up. It couldn't pull into the courtyard because of all the bodies, so it backed up to the gate, and we had to pass the bodies along like a bucket brigade until someone could throw them into the van. While I was carrying the first body, all of a sudden a Kapo who was sitting at a table shouted: 'Hey, her heart just fell out!' I looked down and saw that the body I was carrying was that of a lovely young girl whose chest had been cut open and whose heart had indeed fallen out. It was the first time I had ever seen a human heart. I picked it up and tossed it into the van along with the body. Then I went to get another corpse. This one had been shot in the back of the head—as was the case with most of the bodies—and blood was still pouring out.

"I picked up another body, this one of a young girl. I recognized her because I had seen her on the day an SS guard had taken her to the bunker. She was a young Polish girl who used to walk with a light, confident step. She had no inkling of the fate in store for her. I dragged her by the legs in order to get her to the van, but I shrank back with horror, for all the thigh muscles had been cut away to the bone. The van held 624 bodies; it came back twice." (90)

"If only the Red Cross ambulances could speak, what unbelievable scenes and conversations they could recount. They were used to transport the sick, the elderly, children, and pregnant women who, it was claimed, were being taken to the hospital but who, nine times out of ten, were either thrown directly into a ditch or were shot first by a killer who murdered with fiendish delight." (57)

"All around the camp there was an enormous ditch into which the SS guards pitched the sick and the elderly. In fact, anyone who happened to be near the ditch was shot by the SS and thrown in." (21)

"One day we had to undress. We were completely naked in 10 below zero weather. Towards 6 o'clock we were led, still naked, to a spot between the kitchen and the outer wall of the camp. We waited. Towards nine o'clock in the evening rumors began to circulate that the SS needed a certain number of bodies. Around 11 o'clock we were gathered together and, in the presence of an officer, who happened to be the Camp Commander's adjutant, conducted to the showers. The adjutant made a joke about his revolver and then shot a few prisoners who got in his way. We then went into the shower room, which was guarded by the SS and the camp police. They turned on the showers, and we stood for half an hour under icy water. Then we were driven out with clubs and cudgels, but many of our comrades had already died under the shower. This procedure was repeated three times, at 11 in the evening and at three and four in the morning.

"At seven in the morning SS guards arrived armed with clubs. The survivors (about 200 of us) were forced to run zigzag between the kitchen wall and the outer camp wall. The idea was that we were supposed to run back and forth between the walls while they beat us with clubs along the way. This perverse game lasted until almost eight in the morning when they complained that things weren't moving along fast enough and went to get some axes. I was lucky enough to survive the carnage. Shortly before eight they finally called a halt to the massacre, but by then we had lost a total of 340 comrades and were now down to 60." (49)

"On the anniversary of the death of Ernst von Rath, approximately 20 Jews were taken from various barracks and promptly executed." (105)

"The Germans stepped up the executions the moment they saw the Jews getting bolder." (100)

"One SS guard, who was drunk but alert, forced us to file past him and remove our hats by way of greeting while he used his revolver to shoot us at random." (39)

"In addition to these daily occurrences, I was witness for two days to a terrifying event. All day long trucks full of dozens of prisoners arrived at high speed from the camp at Schirmeck. These prisoners had their hands tied behind their backs. The truck stopped behind the crematory. We heard gunshots. Then the bodies were pitched into an oven whose 40 foot-high chimney glowed red and was so overheated that in the night you could see flames shooting 20 feet high above the chimney top.

"According to reliable information and judging by the number of trips the trucks made, at least 360 people were cremated in this purge. This news, plus the nauseating stench that came from the overheated ovens, spread terror throughout the camp." (88)

"The head of this division was a sadist. He boasted that he could not sit down to dinner until he had killed at least four or five victims." (68)

"For political prisoners and partisans brought into the camp, the Germans preferred a bullet in the neck.

"From the window of the clinic on the second floor of Block 21, we could see what was happening in the courtyard between Blocks 10 and 11. As a matter of fact, I worked in this section of Block 21. Through holes in the curtain we could follow, unnoticed, the executions that were being carried out in the following manner: Two of the men condemned to death were held naked by a prisoner whose job it was to grab them by the arms and drag them at full speed to the black wall. There an SS guard, using a gun with a silencer, would shoot them in the back of the head." (86)

"Our job consisted of getting rid of the bodies and washing away the blood." (82)

"The courtyard was set up for the execution of new victims. As soon as one whole group was liquidated, the bodies would begin arriving at Block 28. By nightfall these bodies, plus those of any other prisoners who had died during the day, were piled on a cart and taken to the ovens." (104)

"With my own eyes I saw 20 bodies pass by, four of them women. They were all Poles. It was our job to haul the bodies in a canvas-covered cart all the way through the camp to the ovens." (82)

"We also filed past some Russians who had been killed. Once they even made us file past a Russian who had been shot but was not yet dead. He died three weeks later in the infirmary." (66)

"A commission from Kattowitz, called the 'Special Court,' spent the night in Block 11. After they were gone, the execution of the victims took place. In September 1942, I watched three boxcars being loaded with the bodies of executed prisoners, 240 in all. On other occasions, the number would be somewhere between 50 and 100. Between the time I arrived at the clinic on July 24, 1942, and January 1945, I saw these executions repeated regularly, usually weekly, but at least twice a month." (86)

"Often three or four SS guards would dress up as doctors and give the appearance of a medical commission. Once some Russians were dragged in and ordered to undress and be examined. Then their heads were pushed under a measuring device that was connected to a trigger. When the measuring stick fell, it depressed the trigger and the victim would be killed by a bullet in the back of the head. The body would then be taken away and the next victim would be brought in. In this way they liquidated between 50 and 100 people who, one by one, entered this room, the walls and floor of which were stained with blood." (71)

"From the window of my squad room, I watched the shooting of a dozen Polish partisans. The SS matrons who were guarding us ordered us not to talk about what we had seen." (61)

"In August 1940, 1,100 new Poles arrived. From the first day on, they were taken in groups to the quarry and shot. After five months, only 300 of them were still alive." (105)

"There was a firing range near the camp exit. One day some Russian prisoners-of-war were led across the camp and brought to this range. A few minutes later you could hear the chatter of machine guns. No one saw the Russian POW's again." (107)

"In another camp, before the ovens had been installed, executions took place in a birch forest and the bodies were burned in ditches. Later, however, executions took place in a large, specially equipped annex of the crematory." (104)

"Out of one group of more than 2,000 Russian POW's, only 80 survived. The others had been either shot or tortured to death. In the winter of 1942, the Germans killed approximately 5,000 Russian POW's. They were taken by truck from the barracks to an abandoned quarry, now a grave, where they were shot and buried. In 1943, 200 Soviet officers arrived at the camp, including two colonels and four majors; the rest were captains and lieutenants. All the officers were shot.

"In 1942, scores of convicts and civilians who had been brought in from outside were shot. Once the SS brought in 88 trucks full of people of all nationalities and ages—men, women, and children—and unloaded them in Krempetz Forest. The victims' clothes and valuables were taken from them and they were shot in front of already dug graves. Mass executions in Krempetz Forest were repeated regularly throughout 1942.

"On one particular spring day of 1942, 6,600 people arrived all at once at the camp. Two days later they were shot. On November 3, 1943, 18,000 were shot, including 8,000 camp inmates and 10,000 people brought in from other camps. Three days before this mass murder occurred, huge ditches had been dug in the open country behind the crematory.

"According to one eyewitness to the mass murder of the Polish population, there were days when 200 to 300 persons or even more were shot.

"A Russian POW by the name of Kneunikow witnessed the execution of 40 women and small children in July 1943. Early in the morning their bodies were taken to the crematory to be burned.

"A witness by the name of Krassovskaya reported to the Polish-Russian Commission that in April 1943, 300 women who had been transported from Greece were shot." (111)

"A low, mucky canal ran through the camp. One cold winter day, a group of Israelis were led in. They were completely naked, women and children, grown-ups and old people. The condemned waded into the water, which came up to their hips. The SS guards gathered at the edge of the canal, sneering at the victims who were trembling with fear and cold. Then they ordered them to dance and sing and jump up and down. They had to sing a specially composed song:

'We are the damned Jews who are destroying the world.'

"They continued to dance and sing for a long time, some for more than two hours, while their bodies sank ever deeper into the muck, but sometimes the Block leaders changed the program. Before the victims sank completely, they would order another group of Israelis to come and pull the dead and dying out of the muck and then carry them away on their shoulders. The newcomers thought they were rescuing some of their fellow-believers, and saving themselves in the process. Weighted down with their burdens, they would back away from the canal. But instead of returning to the barracks, they had to take the bodies to the ovens where, quite literally, the living went to their graves with the dead and dying on their shoulders. This pastime lasted as long as it amused the Block leaders and the other SS guards." (104)

"One day hordes of people were led to the slaughterhouse. The SS said they were Jews and scoundrels and ordered us to beat them with rifle butts. Few of us obeyed this order, for even the meanest could see that these were mostly women and old people.

"Behind the barracks, in the direction of Zutowice, was a big stretch of hilly land. By blasting into a hillside, they carved out a big cave, and the massacre began. The people were lined up in rows of ten. The SS Sergeant who performed the executions wrote down the names, or acted as if he did, and told them that they were receiving the death penalty for sabotage. All were stripped, men and women, and then led to the cave in the side of the hill. A few heavy machine guns were placed in front of them, a few salvos were fired, and the people collapsed. Then the next ones were lined up, and when the area was too full of the dead and wounded, they dynamited the hillside, burying both. Afterwards, the butchers climbed all over this new hill to make sure that no one was left alive.

"I was posted as a guard at the edge of the area. Today my ears still ring with the cries of those unfortunate people, the young women with their children in their arms and the young girls, so full of life, who were murdered by these bloodthirsty brutes, their eyes bulging under the influence of the vodka that let them forget their crimes." (5)

"In this camp there was a room 40 feet long and 20 feet wide where people were strangled. The condemned were never allowed the mercy of a noose, which would simply have broken their necks. Instead, they hung suspended from a metal cable, which slowly strangled them. If, after 20 minutes, they were still alive, they would be beaten with a club." (56)

"Under the ovens there was a large room that served as a morgue and could hold as many as 500 bodies. It was also used for hangings. On the walls of this room were 52 hooks from which victims were suspended. The equipment was quite primitive, and prisoners died more often from suffocation than from strangulation. The executions were performed by two common German criminals in the presence of several SS guards who were present to confirm the deaths.

"The conduct of the prisoners who died in the morgue left no doubt that they knew what they were dying for, and this certainty gave meaning to their lives and to their deaths. I saw a Russian soldier go bravely to his death knowing he had fulfilled his military duty. A Frenchman called out, 'Vive la France'; an Englishman, 'May England live forever'; a Russian, 'Long live the Soviet fatherland.'" (90)

"Finally the 'ideal' room. Those condemned to death were taken immediately to a little door at the far end of the wall where it joined the crematory. This door opened inward until it came in contact with an electrical switch (the kind used to hold a door open) and thus created a corridor 4 feet wide and 3 feet high. At the other end was a 4-foot by 4-foot opening in the floor directly above a concrete shaft 12 feet deep that emptied into the strangulation room. The condemned prisoners were pushed into this shaft where they dropped the 12 feet to the concrete floor below. The moment they hit the floor, the victims were gagged by the SS guards and hung up on hooks along the wall about six feet above the floor.

"There were 45 hooks. When a load of prisoners was to be hanged, those who tried to protect themselves were beaten with a club. (The club and the noose were in the custody of the head of the hospital.) The bodies remained on the hooks until the cremation squad came and got them. An electric elevator, with a capacity of 18 bodies, would rise to the cremation chamber, which was directly above the strangulation chamber. The daily contingent of 200 bodies was made up of approximately 120 prisoners who had died in the infirmary, in the medical experimentation building, or in the so-called 'mini-camp' [Kleinlager], plus the 60 to 80 bodies supplied from the strangulation chamber." (106)

"The gallows were used so often that they became a familiar sight to us. A prisoner could be hanged for an incautious remark, for careless work that was viewed as sabotage, for socializing that was seen as conspiracy, for taking bread from the storeroom, etc. The SS guards turned the executions into a party." (31)

"The condemned were hanged by SS guards in the presence of the mayor of the village, the police, and the members of their squad, while other SS personnel armed with machine pistols stood guard." (105)

"You could hear the camp music celebrating the glory of the Reich as the last victim in a row of 30 was executed.

"In the tunnel the procedure was given a particularly spectacular twist: 20 condemned prisoners were tied by the neck to an electric hoist. At the push of a button, the 20 victims arose simultaneously into the air high over the floor, under the eyes of all the assembled workers in the tunnel. Immediately afterwards the workers were made to file past their hanged comrades and were told not to avert their eyes if they didn't want to receive a severe beating." (31)

"Three days before my arrival the SS guards ordered a German prisoner, a common criminal, to hang a young Polish prisoner. It was a public hanging. The German kicked him and he fell, but the rope was so long that his feet touched the earth. No one moved to help him. The procedure was repeated until he finally died." (21)

"In retaliation for unspecified incidents that had taken place outside the camp, Poles were again singled out to be hanged for all to see. Once they hanged 21 at the same time." (105)

"I was also present at the hanging of six prisoners, all Communists (four Germans and two Poles) who, at the moment of hanging, put up considerable resistance. One kicked a certain SS liaison officer, the meanest one in the camp. Just before they died, they cried out: 'Down with Hitler's Germany!' 'Hail Soviet Russia!' 'Down with SS barbarianism!' 'Long live Poland!'" (86)

"In August 1944, a number of Allied paratroopers arrived at the camp. The method of processing them was always the same: Their names would be called out upon arrival, they would be locked up for the night, and the next day they would be taken to the crematory where they would first be hanged. The paratroopers were English, American, and French. The Kapo who was in charge of the internees had to be able to provide an exact count." (38)

"34 English and Canadian pilots were hanged at the beginning of September 1944." (105)

"One day 37 English and French members of the Intelligence Service arrived at the camp and were assigned to Block 7. They were not put to work. We didn't know their fate until one day when 16 of them were called out and didn't return. I found out that evening that all of them had been hanged. I requested proof, and my friend from the crematory brought me notebooks and various papers belonging to them. Then we knew for sure the fate that awaited the others. I tried to save these 21 people, but in a concentration camp it was not easy. A friend of mine from Amsterdam (J. R.) and I decided to get ourselves an SS uniform and try to get these men out of the camp as if they had been freed.

"I already had the necessary green papers for exiting the camp. All I lacked was the stamp of a certain political department, a stamp which another friend was supposed to secure. Meanwhile, J. R. had been able to get hold of an SS uniform. Unfortunately, we found out one evening that 17 of these prisoners had been ordered to fall out the following morning at 6 o'clock.

"There was nothing else for us to do but try to prepare these poor fellows for death, which we did with the help of a French priest. They were all shot, but before they died, they shouted, 'Long live our homeland and freedom!' Only four prisoners in this group were left to save, two English and two French. All four received a light injection of exanthematic typhus and were immediately taken to the typhus station in Block 46.

"A week later, four French prisoners, who had served as guinea pigs, died in Block 46. We exchanged the names of our four prisoners with those of the four dead Frenchmen whose names we turned over to the Intelligence Service. It was my job to hand over corpses to the nearest crematory before the SS doctor could find out about the switch. Everything went well and the last four prisoners were saved." (90)

"In the prison there were hangings every day. Seven gallows had been erected there, and they were in operation full- or part-time almost daily. For example, they would take people out of a squad and hang them, taking them away from their work in order to execute them. There was never any sort of reason given for these executions, which were carried out in total secrecy. For example, one day in August 1944 they came and got a carpenter, right in the middle of his work, and hanged him along with 36 others prisoners. Toward the end of my stay, sometime in February 1945, they hanged 60 Dutch prisoners who had recently arrived from Holland and had belonged to the resistance movement. We didn't know any of the details of their case. I was working at that time as an orderly and was called in to take down six of these Dutch prisoners from the gallows. Seven of them were hanged every 20 minutes. When they were pronounced dead, a new group would be executed.

"One of my comrades, who was behind bars at the time, told me that from his cell he could hear hangings taking place all the time.

"In the beginning the hangings were performed by a camp senior (one of the prisoners who had been there the longest). This man (a political prisoner) was replaced during the winter (when he joined the SS) by another senior, a man who was even shrewder. He knew how to find three other Block seniors who would volunteer to act as executioners." (73)

"All this killing was organized administratively according to specific regulations; all the particulars were straight out of the camp archives. All results of these procedures were written down in careful account ledgers. Regular reports were made to the higher authorities. Everything was done strictly 'by the book.'

"As a matter of fact, every week the Camp Kommandant sent his superiors standardized forms on which numerical postings of the week's dead were separated into five categories: those who died from sickness, those who were shot, those who were hanged, those who hanged themselves (with a rope supplied to them), and those who committed suicide some other way." (65)

"The list of the murdered camp prisoners grew constantly through the number of Russian POW's; through various population groups brought from occupied European countries; through population groups whom the Gestapo had apprehended on the streets, in railroad stations, in their homes, during raids; and through house searches conducted by the Nazis methodically in Poland and other European countries; and finally, by those Jews taken from the ghettos and handed over by the Gestapo in Poland as well as various western European cities.

"Among the prisoners were countless women, children, and old people. Sometimes the prisoners constituted a whole family. There were children of all ages, even babies." (111)

"A German prisoner named Karr was charged by the SS guards with giving lethal injections. In principle he was supposed to inject only the incurable. Actually every morning he chose those who had not given him their [Red Cross] packages, young boys who would not have anything to do with his depraved tastes, and others simply at random. He notified them at morning roll call, but they didn't get the injection until evening so that they would have the whole day to think about death and reflect on their fate." (63)

"I myself know of a top surgeon of the hospital who was given a lethal dose of phenol in the heart because he complained.

"Young Aryans, mostly young Russians, who had been arrested with their parents as partisans in Russia, along with young Poles who arrived at the camp with their parents, whether they were political prisoners or partisans, were divided into three groups of 50 to 60 each and led into the courtyard of Block 20. There they had to undress on the grounds that they were to be medically examined and given a shower. These children were led two at a time into the laboratory where they received an injection of phenol in the heart." (86)

"Here I saw several women arrive, at least two of whom were English. Another two were certainly French. The SS guards took them into the bunker and murdered them in the night with injections, after which they undressed them." (21)

"This was one way of getting rid of people who mouthed off." (86)

"Together with Madame B., a Belgian woman from Ostende, I saw the following scene being played out: In front of us, the SS doctor asked Mlle. B., a 21 year-old Belgian journalist, the reason for her presence in the camp. She replied that she had many Boche to thank for her death, whereupon the doctor told her to go to the infirmary and ordered the nurse who was with us to 'escort' her. That same day Mlle. B. received a medication to drink, a brown fluid from which she died a few hours later." (92)

"During the last week, 12 people were brought to the cellblock to await execution. I tried to console them by telling them that the Nazi rule was coming to an end and that the Nazis didn't have time enough left to kill them all. But it didn't work out that way. On April 25 big changes occurred. They were put two each in separate cells. It was about this same time that the coffee pot mysteriously disappeared. I looked everywhere for it, but I couldn't find it, so I took another pot. But when I walked into the cell where the crematory workers lived, Frau Inspector Nowes handed me the missing pot and ordered me to pour them coffee. I didn't think anything of it at the moment and started pouring coffee for the prisoners. Then it suddenly occurred to me that the coffee might be poisoned. The Frau Inspector called me over, grabbed the pot out of my hands, and finished pouring the coffee for the prisoners herself.

"At 10 o'clock they collected the bodies. We had to disappear. Everything was eerily quiet. We didn't know anything and went back to work. At noon an SS guard volunteered to help distribute the food. He took his time and asked me to carry the kettle. He went directly to Cell 47 where these people were and said to me: 'Dish out the food to them.' It was clear to me that the people had assumed that the coffee was probably poisoned (and that's why they had not drunk it) and that there was also poison in the food. The SS guard looked at me amazed and angry. He asked me what I knew. Then he went away, and so did I. He came back later and dished out the food himself.

"Two of the people had not noticed anything and had gone ahead and eaten. By evening they were dead. That same evening I was supposed to dish out the food again. I looked into Cell 47 and asked if they wanted to eat. They all said, 'Yes,' if I would serve it to them. They were very upset and thought that they were going to be killed. I was very upset myself and calmed them by saying that the end of the Nazis was almost there and that I would testify for them. I regret that I did not get the names of these people. From their way of speaking they were Poles and Germans.

"The next morning we discovered what we had feared. The cell was empty, all were gone. Only traces remained to show that they had been butchered. There was a mallet lying on a table and a blood spot they had tried to cover up with black soil. Even so, the shed was splattered with blood, including the walls. Everything had happened that the crematory workers had feared would happen. They had been murdered so that there would be no witnesses to the horrible deeds of these tyrants." (31)

"It is true that tattooed prisoners were murdered and their skin tanned. I myself saw this happen to 200 prisoners who at the very moment of their liberation, as they were about to board the evacuation trucks, were executed because of their tattoos. In order to preserve the freshness of their tattoos, the executioners made haste to remove the skin before the body turned cold." (47)

"It was the wife of an SS officer who popularized this method. Every tattooed prisoner was brought to her. If she found his tattoo to her taste, the prisoner would be killed and the skin removed. Then the skin would be tanned and made into mementos (lamp shades, wall hangings, book bindings, etc.). Apparently, 40 samples of these artistic products were found by 1st Lieutenant Walter F. Emmos. We ourselves saw six such samples in the general staff room of the camp, including a lamp shade." (106)

"Between May 1941 and February 1943, the camp was occupied three times by approximately 8,000 people; during the same time 21,000 died or were murdered. In January 1943, the average daily death toll reached 100." (112)

"21,200 Dutch Jews were delivered to the camp, then taken to Güsen near Mauthausen where, to the last man, they were liquidated." (105)

"A number of priests were buried alive up to their necks while the SS guards smashed their skulls with stones, drove heavy wheelbarrows over their heads, and forced the other prisoners, under penalty of death, to do the same." (40)

"The death toll in the camps in February and March 1943 amounted to between 500 and 600 people per day out of 10,000 to 12,000 deportees. One day when there were only 12 deaths, an SS guard remarked: 'So few?' People who were in the camp for the purpose of being gassed were not included in that number." (35)

"There was one terrible day, a day that I cannot erase from my memory, a day that I do not want to ignore with silence. During the four days that preceded this day, the Jews of the concentration camp were forced to dig ditches next to the crematory, allegedly for an antiaircraft battery. Unfortunately, these ditches turned out to be their graves.

"On that day the guard was tripled. Field V and the infirmary were both evacuated. All the Jews—men, women, and children, as well as the half-Jews—were led between two rows of police to Field V. I was right by Field V, and they had to file right past me. All day long they passed by in double time. Those who couldn't keep up were butchered on the spot by the police. Jews were brought here from all over, from camps in Lublin, Pulawn, Cholm, Zamese, etc.

"When the Jews arrived at Field V, they had to undress; then they were taken to the ditches. They were told to lie down next to each other in the ditches. Then the Security Police (SD) and the Gestapo gunned them down with machine guns. Others had to lie down on top of the dead, then still others on top of them, layer upon layer, until the ditch was full. Then the whole thing would happen all over again in another ditch. In order to drown out the noise of the machine guns, powerful loudspeakers broadcast deafening music. 18,000 Jews went to their death on that day." (60)

"The Germans called this mass execution 'special treatment' ('Sonderbehandlung'). And under this label a report was sent to Berlin. This report said literally: 'The difference between the number of internees this morning and those this evening is based on the special extermination of 18,000 persons.'" (111)

Chapter 10

Impact on the Prisoners

REVOLT - FLIGHT - SUICIDE

"Never a revolt. The demoralization was such that you mistrusted your neighbor, and there were not enough of us to try to resist." (23)

"The greater the misery, the greater the disunity among the prisoners." (10)

"The dirty clothes, the beatings, the collective punishment, the crude but effective propaganda that stirred up animosity among the inmates, the mixed nationalities in crowded compounds, the near impossibility of washing (8 washbasins for 500 people), the constant turnover of people in the compound or the workplace as a way of preventing the formation of close friendships—all of it worked together to demoralize people left on their own in a miserable, hostile environment, to humiliate them, and to abandon them to despair." (63)

"Sporadic attempts at revolt or at mass escape while disembarking from the boxcars were savagely suppressed. The railroad platform reserved for these shipments was surrounded by floodlights and machine guns. Once, however, the prisoners chalked up a minor success. It happened in either September or October 1943, following the arrival of a shipment of women. The accompanying SS guards had ordered them to undress, and they were on the verge of being taken to the gas chamber. It was at this moment that the guards took the opportunity to rob the women by yanking rings and watches from the their hands and wrists. During the ensuing confusion, one woman managed to grab a pistol from SS Group Leader Schillinger and fire three shots at him. He was seriously wounded and died the next day. For the others that was the signal to attack the hangmen and their cohorts. One SS guard had his nose torn off, another was scalped, but unfortunately not one woman managed to escape." (104)

"At that point, the SS guards launched a full-scale attack. That evening the SS guards stormed into the camp in a blind rage and fired at the prisoners at random. There were 13 dead, 4 badly wounded, and 31 slightly wounded." (86)

"It should also be pointed out that those prisoners who worked in the Special Squad (the squad assigned to the ovens) tried twice to revolt. The first time was in 1942. The squad consisted of about 200 men who planned to kill their guards, confiscate their weapons, and attempt to flee. Unfortunately, they were denounced by one of their own comrades and shot.

"The second uprising took place in September 1944 at the time of a massive shipment from Hungary. The Special Squad consisted at that time of 800 persons. The revolt was timed to take place on a Friday and coincide with the arrival of a load of internees. Weapons supplied by the Polish resistance movement were supposed to arrive at the camp on same day. Unfortunately, the internees scheduled to arrive on Friday arrived two days early. Even without weapons, the members of the Special Squad decided to resist anyway by locking themselves in the crematory. Almost all of them were annihilated." (29)

"There was also a sort of bond between the French and the anti-Fascists of all countries. Thanks to this brotherhood, I survived." (23)

"The 'habitat' of the prisoners, if one can use this expression, was an area in the inner camp that measured about 300 by 500 yards. It was surrounded by a double row of 10-foot-high concrete posts, which were connected by a double network of high-tension wires that were attached to the posts by insulators." (104)

"This electrical system had not yet been put into operation. The barbed-wire fencing had been there from the start but without electrical current. The electric plant was set up as a result of of the following incident: In May 1942, a group of Russian POW's, who had been sent to the Krempetz Forest not far from the camp to bury the dead, had killed seven German guards with shovels and escaped. Two of these prisoners were caught, but the other 15 were able to elude their pursuers. In retaliation, the 130 POW's still alive in the camp (out of the 1,000 prisoners who had arrived in August 1941) were taken to the same compound the others had escaped from. Since they knew that they were going to die anyway, the Russian POW's decided, with the exception of a dozen or so, to break out. One evening toward the end of June they took their blankets, laid them five deep over the barbed wire, and using them as a bridge, climbed over the wire and fled. The night was dark. Four of them were killed; the others succeeded in getting away. After this escape, the 50 prisoners who remained in the camp were led immediately into the courtyard, knocked to the ground, and machine gunned. But that was not enough to satisfy the Germans.

There remained the embarrassment of a successful escape. So they electrified the barbed wire." (110)

"One woman who tried to escape got stuck on the fence and died." (43)

"Between the two rows of posts, 150 yards apart, were five tall watchtowers equipped with machine guns and floodlights. In front, at the inner circle of high tension wires, was a barrier of ordinary wire. Just to touch this barrier would trigger a hail of bullets from the the watchtowers. This set-up was called 'the little chain' or 'the inner chain of sentries.' The camp itself consisted of three rows of buildings. Between the first and second rows was the main camp street, and between the second and the third rows there stretched a wall.

"Within a radius of approximately 2,000 yards, the camp complex was enclosed by a second line (called 'the big chain' or 'outer chain') of sentries, which contained watchtowers positioned 150 yards apart. Between the inner and outer chains were the factories and other work facilities. The watchtowers of the inner chain were manned only at night when the high-tension wires in the double rows were electrified. During the day, the garrison of the inner chain was pulled back, and the people did their jobs within the outer chain.

"Although many attempts were made, escape between the watchtowers was virtually impossible. And it was absolutely impossible to get through the inner post line at night. The towers of the outer chain were so close to each other (a tower every 150 yards, with an average of 75 yards per tower to be watched over) that there could be no question of coming near without being noticed. The garrison of the outer chain was pulled back at dusk, but only after they were sure that all prisoners were securely inside the inner chain.

"If a prisoner turned up missing at roll call, the sirens would immediately sound the alarm. The guards in the outer chain would then remain on alert in the towers while the inner chain would be occupied by more guards and hundreds of SS personnel, and the police dogs would begin a systematic search. The sirens could be heard throughout the surrounding countryside so that if, amazingly enough, an escapee did somehow manage to get through the outer chain, he could be fairly certain of being caught by one of the many German police patrols or by the SS. Besides, an escapee was handicapped by his shaved head, his striped prison clothes, the patches sewed on his clothes, and the passivity of the thoroughly frightened populace. If the prisoner was still not caught, the garrison of the outer chain would remain on alert for three days and three nights." (104)

"In spite of the virtual impossibility of escape, attempts were made from time to time." (121)

"During our two-year imprisonment, countless attempts were made to escape, but with the exception of two or three, all who tried were brought back dead or alive. We never did know whether those two or three who were not brought back had truly managed to escape. But we can say that, of the Jews who were deported to our camp from Czechoslovakia, we were the only ones who were lucky enough to be rescued." (104)

"Whenever anybody escaped, those who stayed behind were punished. All the internees, sick, old, or weak, were forced to perform group exercises, like running in double time, crawling on the floor, etc., and during these exercises the camp chief, the camp leader, and the assistant leader, as well as those supervisors chosen from among the German prisoners, beat us with metal clubs and rubber truncheons.

"A 62-year-old man with terminal heart disease, who was unable to run, begged for mercy and collapsed on the floor. The brutes fell upon him in a rage, beat him mercilessly, and forced him to continue with the exercises. The next day he was dead." (4)

"If an escapee was found dead, his body would be brought back to the camp (it was easy to identify the bodies by means of the tattoos) and propped up at the entrance with a sign in his hand that said: 'Here I am.' If he was found alive, he would be executed in front of the whole camp." (104)

"One day a Russian prisoner escaped, but they caught him and dragged him to our compound where they tortured him before our very eyes. They burned the soles of his feet. He fell on his knees. They ordered him to stand up. The SS guards hit him with their belts. The blows broke his spine and one eye fell out of its socket. The victim was perhaps 30 years old. His fight against death lasted all night. We could hear him moaning." (28)

"Another Russian prisoner was caught trying to escape and was shot down in cold blood 300 yards from the camp.

"They turned the dogs loose on two Poles who tried to escape. One was killed, the other survived, but as a result of the bites, he sustained severe wounds. The camp leader had the survivor tied to his dead comrade and ordered the whole camp to file past. Some Frenchmen who filed past and tried to speak to the victims received several lashes with a bullwhip.

"The wounded man was tied to his dead comrade for 48 hours, during which time he was lashed with the bullwhip at the slightest sign of weakness. His wounds got worse, but he continued to be tied to the dead man. Then he was taken to the prison where he died under horrible circumstances. He looked like a mound of rotting flesh." (16)

"One of my comrades experienced the death of her husband who, with five or six other prisoners, had tried to flee. They were left naked in the snow for eight days, but her husband died in six." (85)

"One Russian prisoner did manage to escape, but unfortunately, he

was found in the square of a neighboring village. The Camp Kommandant went there and gathered the entire population of the village
together. Then he ordered the Russian to come forward and completely
undress, whereupon he used his own whip to beat the man until he bled.
Finally he finished him off with a bullet in the head. After he had
committed this murder, he had the body strapped to his car so he could
haul it back to the camp and show it off to the prisoners." (116)

"One night six men succeeded in reaching the barbed-wire fence and
began to climb over. They were spotted in the glare of the floodlights
by the guards in the watchtower and surrendered on the spot. In the
meantime a sentry had been alerted and, in spite of their begging and
pleading, he gunned them down without batting an eye. We all witnessed this scene, which was brightly lit by floodlights." (50)

"In September 1944, a French lieutenant named B. was hanged in
Neckargerach because of an escape attempt. A minute and a half after
the hanging, the SS noticed that B. was still alive, so they took clubs
and beat on his skull until it was crushed and they were sure he was
completely dead." (105)

"I witnessed many hangings which were the result of attempts to
escape." (110)

"In October 1943, a number of Czechs dug a tunnel in order to escape.
These Czechs were captured at the very moment their plan was about to
be put into effect. On a Saturday afternoon we were assembled in the
central courtyard of the camp and were surprised to see a lot of tables
pushed together over which X-shaped racks had been erected. These
supported posts from which 17 nooses were suspended. These were the
gallows that were prepared for the hanging of the Czechs who had
been brought from Auschwitz.

"They had to stand on the tables and stick their heads in the nooses.
The whole camp witnessed this spectacle. The Kapos and the German
and Polish Block leaders were instructed to kick over the tables. The
victims of the execution were extremely brave and died crying: 'Down
with Naziism' and 'Long live freedom.'" (87)

"I also witnessed the hanging of a Czechoslovakian Jew who had
tried to escape three times. After the third try he was sentenced to be
hanged, but fortunately for him the rope broke. The prisoner who had
secured the rope was accused of sabotage. The whole camp awaited the
pardon of the prisoner, but at 9 o'clock in the evening a yellow truck
arrived at the compound and took him away. 25 hours later we found
out in the registration room that his name had disappeared from the
camp's supply list." (110)

"In September 1944, I witnessed the hanging of a Russian who had
tried to escape. This hanging was performed in an unusual way: the
victim stood on a stool with the noose around his neck. The SS guard,

who held the end of the rope, kicked the stool aside and death occurred from strangulation, for the body of the prisoner was no more than eight inches off the floor. The SS guard knew without a doubt that death had resulted in this way, for he looked at his watch and ordered us (there were 150 of us) to behold this spectacle for a quarter of an hour, without once averting our eyes. We were forced to observe the thrashing legs, the bulging eyes, and the protruding tongue." (88)

"Once three internees who tried to escape were caught. It was on a Saturday. The next morning at 3 a.m. we were summoned to roll call. In the courtyard, in front of all the assembled internees, a gallows was erected, and the three victims were hanged. All the internees were ordered to stand at attention all day Sunday until sundown without taking their eyes off the three who had been hanged. Anyone who fainted or moved out of line was shot on the spot." (121)

"The very act of neglecting to give information about the actions of a prisoner or, worse yet, of helping one was punishable by death." (104)

"Because of an escape attempt by three men, a squad of 12 engineers of various nationalities was hanged in July 1943: Poles, Czechs, Hungarians, and maybe a Dutchman." (40)

"On Sunday, September 12, we had to stand at attention from 6 a.m. until noon in the courtyard because a Russian prisoner, in spite of the barbed wire, the electric fence, and the two watch towers, had been successful in escaping from the camp. We never found out how he had managed it. A friend of the escaped prisoner was tied all afternoon to a post and then shot. The reason given was that he knew the intentions of his comrade and didn't tell anyone.

"The Block leader was found hanged in the tool room. He was hanged on orders, but officially the following version was given out: 'Aware that he had violated his duty in abetting the escape of a prisoner and in trying to avoid his deserved punishment, he simply hanged himself.'" (60)

"One escape attempt resulted in the condemning of all the escapee's 16 roommates." (106)

"When an engineer, a Polish internee in the construction office, escaped, the Germans selected 12 hostages from among those who worked in the same office and hanged them." (110)

"I was often in the depths of despair and wanted to hang myself, but my cellmate advised me not to do it and not to be a coward. I took his advice to heart and looked upon it as a miracle that I survived." (38)

"It is only natural, given the sort of treatment they endured, that it would make sense for a person to find quick death a solution. That's why suicides were so common." (96)

"To end their suffering, many prisoners took their own lives by leaping into a 400- to 600-foot-deep quarry." (112)

"Many of them went mad when they found out that their children had been cremated and threw themselves against the electrified barbed wire." (18)

"Most of the ones who committed suicide did so by hurling themselves against the high tension wires of the inner fence." (104)

"Once when a female internee ran into the electrified barbed wire while trying to flee from an SS matron who was beating her, the guard made the other women prisoners file past the body as she asked: 'Who's next?'" (48)

"An average of 50 women died per day either from privation or by flinging themselves against the electrified barbed wire that encircled the entire camp." (113)

After Himler (left) visited Auschwitz in 1942, the decision was made to use gas for mass extermination

A mass grave

Dead children look eerily like their confiscated dolls

Dolls of slain children bear a macabre resemblance to bodies in an open grave

Assorted trinkets ghoulishly pilfered from the dead

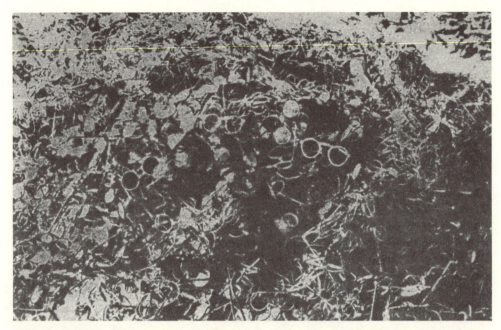

Thousands of pairs of confiscated eyeglasses bear witness to the fate of their owners and the callousness of their executioners

A rare view inside a gas chamber piled high with dead bodies awaiting cremation

Chapter 11

Extermination

"It was after Himmler's visit to Auschwitz on July 17, 1942 (I saw him myself) that the decision was made to use gas for mass extermination.

"For this purpose special 'gas barracks' were built, huge airtight chambers that were equipped with vents that could be opened or closed as needed. Inside they were furnished like baths in order to fool the victims." (104)

"Before stationary gas chambers were constructed, there were mobile ones that consisted of sealed trucks in which 10 to 12 persons were gassed. A can of 'Zyklon' would be tossed inside, and the prisoners would be dead in 10 to 12 minutes.

"The gas chambers consisted of two rooms. In one the prisoners undressed, and in the other they were gassed." (86)

"The new arrivals who were to be gassed undressed in the waiting room. This room was a model of Hitlerian hypocrisy and lies. It was luxuriously appointed, and there were clothes hangers along the walls with enameled plates above them that bore the following message in various languages: 'If you want to find your clothes again as you leave, be sure to remember your number.'" (57)

"On the walls there were signs with the words 'Disinfection' and 'Bath' in various languages.

"After undressing in the first room, the prisoners would carefully gather their clothes together in bundles so that they could find them again on their way out. A sign also instructed them to take a towel and soap; then they were led into the gas chamber." (86)

"A large room adjoined the first. It was about 30 feet long, 20 to 25 feet wide, and 15 to 20 feet high. Running the length of the upper part of the room were two perforated tubes through which the gas was pumped in." (82)

"'Zyklon' gas was chosen by the Germans after a trial run in Lublin and one in Auschwitz on October 25, 1941, in which 800 Russian POW's were herded into the basement of Block XI and gassed. Two days later, 600 Poles, among whom were several high-ranking officers, were gassed in the same place. Then, in the chambers of Crematory No. 1, even smaller experiments were performed on anywhere from 50 to 100 persons. An ambulance with Red Cross insignia delivered the gas in metal containers." (102)

"Distinguished visitors from Berlin attended the opening of the first crematory in March 1943. On the 'program' was the gassing and burning of 8,000 Jews from Krakow. The visitors—officers and civilians alike—were extremely satisfied with the results, and the window that had been specially installed in the door of the gas chamber was constantly in use. The visitors were full of praise for this latest novelty." (104)

"Extermination by means of gas was used primarily on those deported on the basis of race (Jews and Gypsies) and on certain political prisoners." (86)

"Those who were taken to the gas chambers were either those who were earmarked for extermination before they even arrived at the train station and were brought directly to the gas chambers, or those unfit to work—the old, the sick, the weak—all of whom were worked to death before being sent to the gas chamber. Also executed in this way were prisoners from other shipments who were singled out by a special sign from the Gestapo." (90)

"The main method of exterminating the sick and the weak before this time was as follows: A small chamber was set up next to the crematory. Its entrance was so low that the prisoners had to bend over to pass through the door. Two SS guards brandishing clubs stood on either side of the door, and when the prisoners ducked to get through, the SS guards would hit them on the head with their iron clubs. If the guard on one side missed, the one on the other side was always there. If the victims didn't die immediately but were just barely unconscious, it didn't matter. They were considered dead and shoved into the oven." (110)

"The Germans also executed people in a car especially designed for that purpose; it was called a 'gas car' ('Gaswagen')." (111)

SELECTION IN THE CAMP

"Every two weeks the SS doctor came to perform what we called 'selection.' The sick would be stripped naked by a Polish 'section leader.'

For hours they had to stand, regardless of their health, while they waited for the arrival of the doctor, who would barely look at them and then take a few patients' charts away with him. Two days later the patients whose charts had been taken away would be driven to an unspecified destination. There the doctor in charge would order us to fill out new forms and enter the cause of death and the date: Mr. X died of____ on____. The cause of death was left up to those filling out the forms." (82)

"Selection took place in the infirmary every week or two." (86)

"Anyone who had typhus or was suspected of having typhus had to die." (35)

"On August 16, 1942, selection of 863 typhus patients took place. In April 1944, another selection claimed 6,000 victims among whom were Jewish women with leprosy." (86)

"There were many young people and sick people who wanted to stay longer in the hospital in order to recover completely but who died suddenly.

"A prisoner came to the infirmary because of a boil, a nonthreatening illness. He was still there when the Commission came through, and he was sent to the gas chamber. He thought he was being taken to another camp and said to me, 'Doctor, we'll meet again in Paris.'

"A Dutchman appeared before the doctor. On his chart it was noted that he usually stayed no longer than five days before he was able to go back to work. The doctor declared that five days for his recovery was not enough time and that it would be at least 15 days before he could return to work. After this had been discussed for a while, he instructed me to put down 15 days. The next day I learned that all those who stayed longer than five days were sent to the gas chamber." (36)

"From among the sick women, they selected those with a fever." (87)

"The sick Israelis and the very sick Aryans were not treated but sent to the gas chamber." (61)

"In Ravensbrück, women who were old and sick were the first to suffer the fate of the gas chamber. The procedure took place one morning in the following way: The doctor arrived, put a cross next to the names of hundreds of patients, and left. A few days later a black, canvas-covered truck driven by SS guards picked up the designated women. Before they had time to dress, they were taken to the gas chamber. This was repeated countless times until the screaming began to permeate the camp." (114)

"Those who had bad skin color or were in bad physical shape were selected for gassing at the whim of the camp doctor. They were then taken to the infirmary where between 40 and 50 percent were 'evacuated.' A 'delousing,' which most victims required, took place in July 1942. In the course of this 'cleansing,' the weak—those with typhus or those who were recuperating from typhus—were all sent to the gas chamber. This method was considered the most extreme." (104)

"The 'Moslems' were those who were so emaciated that their work was no longer considered productive." (3)

"For the men and boys, selection took place inside the Blocks. Selection for the women (except for those in the infirmary) usually took place outside because it was more degrading for women or young girls to stand completely naked for hours on end in full view of everyone, including the men who worked in the women's camps.

"When selection was announced, the order would be given for all interned women to gather completely naked in the area between the Blocks. As soon as they had assembled, a 'Blockova' would lead them, in columns of four, to the big courtyard next to the kitchen. There the selection process would begin in the presence of the chief physician, who was sometimes accompanied by the camp Kommandant, but was more often alone. The unfortunate women would tremble with cold and fear as they filed past him at a distance of six paces. As they passed by, the executioner would decide their fate. With his arm outstretched and his fist clenched, he would move his thumb to the right or to the left. Those who went to the left were those selected to be gassed and burned, those to the right side were allowed to return to their compounds." (57)

"Sometimes they would come to the women's compound after working hours and have the internees file past them, or they might do it in the morning at roll call." (41)

"Selection was made without any regard whatsoever for age or constitution. Robust or feeble, young or old, pretty or haggard from sorrow, trouble, or fear—there was no distinction made." (57)

"Selection could be made on the basis of age, hair color, or swollen legs, or maybe whether a woman was able to run or not." (41)

"Those who didn't please them, because their clothes were dirty or for some such reason, would be sentenced to extermination even if they were strong and completely healthy." (94)

"If no one else was left to be gassed, they would choose their victims from among the Jewish women in the camp.

"In this best of all possible administrative machines only the numbers counted. It so happened that one patient selected to be gassed the next day died in the infirmary a day early. Since this would botch the statistics, his body was held back and then sent to the gas chamber the next day so that it would be included with the others being delivered to the crematory where a final count took place." (102)

"[As a doctor] I tried to protect many women either by letting them slip out the window, or by changing their numbers, or hiding them under a mattress, or by falsifying their temperature charts." (32)

"I witnessed horrible scenes of desperation. There was no end to the screaming, the crying, the moaning, to the suicide attempts, or to every manner of praying. Never will I be able to forget these poor wretches who with horror faced their death sentences." (57)

"The Jewish holidays, like the Jewish New Year and Yom Kippur, were the occasions for the selection of Hungarian Jews to be sent to the crematory." (82)

"2,000 people believed they were going to America, but instead of going to America, they were taken to the gas chamber." (35)

"There was also another way to get rid of the prisoners who were in quarantine. It consisted of asking which of them felt too weak for heavy work and would like to go on 'chicken coop' detail. Many signed up for this, but instead of being put on the detail in question, they were sent to the gas chamber." (90)

"On more than one occasion, feeble-minded old women were asked if they felt sick or weak because, if so, they would be given milk. When they said yes, their numbers were added to the black list and the poor things went to their death." (122)

"An average of 1,000 persons were selected per week. If the compound was overcrowded, the evacuation to the gas chamber was speeded up." (35)

"And while, with a flick of the wrist, the doctor decided the fate of hundreds and thousands of people, he would whistle or hum opera tunes to himself." (57)

"When they selected children, they measured them first and then sent them to the gas chamber according to size. The doctor made his decision by using a yardstick. Those who were more than three feet tall were spared, and the others went to the gas chamber." (35)

"The camp doctor, an SS lieutenant, told me on the evening of October 21, 1943, that on this day 300 children between the ages of 3 and 10 had been gassed with the preparation known as 'Zyklon.'" (111)

"There was even a squad of young girls whose job it was to undress the children selected for gassing. This squad was called 'The White Gowns.' It is not difficult to imagine their state of mind. If they resisted, they were sent to the gas chamber themselves. Through terror these people were forced to cremate their own comrades." (103)

"The extermination of Gypsy children began in April 1943. One day the chief physician asked the Kommandant, 'How many children do you have here?' '4,000,' was the answer. 'You have 2,000 too many. Send the others to the baths.' The next morning half of them were gassed." (94)

"The means of transportation to the place of execution varied; it depended on the mood of the executioner. If he decided that these unfortunate women should be transported immediately, the trucks came and they were squeezed in, standing 80 to 100 per truck. If it was nightfall, a human procession was formed and the prisoners were dispatched on foot to the crematory, surrounded by a great many SS guards who were prepared for a bloodbath at the least sign of an escape attempt. Also, if the women were not properly lined up, they were struck down. Sometimes they were taken away in groups of 2,000 or 3,000 or even more." (57)

"Sometimes, when an execution day was scheduled, they would seal off all Blocks the night before. Then all the patients would be gathered together to wait for the arrival of the trucks that would transport them to the gas chambers which were not more than 500 yards from the hospital." (35)

"In 1942 the administration proceeded quite differently. The moment the prisoners arrived, there was a truck ready to take them to the ovens." (12)

"The selected had to climb aboard the truck where the dead women were mixed in with the living." (41)

"With machine pistols in their hands, the SS would force the victims to climb aboard. The Jews were often quite brave. They would curse the SS and prophesy a similar death for them, saying: 'Your women and children will die a wretched death like us.'" (35)

"I saw women being sent to the gas chambers who knew they were doomed and who, dressed only in a chemise, their number tattooed on their arms, were squeezed into a truck." (32)

"The way those who were condemned to be gassed were apprised of their fate was extraordinarily cruel and inhumane. Patients who had just had surgery and were still wearing bandages, patients who were exhausted and emaciated, patients who were convalescing but far from well were all loaded on trucks. They were naked, and the sight was absolutely appalling. The trucks stood at the entrance to the compound, and the poor victims were simply thrown onto them or packed into them. I was too often an eyewitness to such misery." (104)

"About a hundred people were squeezed into a small truck. All knew exactly the fate that awaited them. The vast majority of them remained absolutely apathetic while others, particularly the patients from the infirmary with their open sores and bleeding wounds, put up fierce resistance. The SS guards raced around the trucks like maniacs, kicking at the howling crowd who tried to draw back. It was always a grueling experience to drag our friends to the trucks. Most of them were quiet and reserved, but they took the opportunity whenever they could to say to us: 'Don't forget to avenge us.' Under such circumstances a person's heart turns to stone. I think of the prisoner who killed his very own brother in one of the sick wards just to spare him the terrible journey in the truck. I know the names and numbers of both these men." (86)

"One shipment had to wait outside until the previous one was taken care of." (35)

"The truck came and went very quickly; it took no more than 5 or 10 minutes for the round trip." (41)

"One Sunday a truck so overloaded it was about to break down made six trips to the sick bay where the women with tuberculosis were kept and took away women who were scarcely sick. On Easter Saturday seven trucks took women to the gas chamber. Among them, according to testimony, was Mother Elsabeth, head mistress of a childrens' home in Lyon." (114)

"Nothing further was said about these women, and a few days later it was reported that they had 'died in the convalescent camp.' That was the official wording." (41)

"And while shipments of innocent people went to the ovens, the orchestra played loud music on the other side of the street." (50)

"Usually 80 percent of the sick were selected. They knew they were going to die, but they were left for 48 more hours in the compound." (32)

"90 percent were taken each day in the barracks where I tended the sick. I cried like a child." (35)

"At a single stroke, approximately 2,000 persons were selected from among the weakest. These people were gassed, then cremated. The largest selection took place on January 1, 1944. 85 percent of the camp population, a population that had been continually replenished, were cremated at that time." (68)

"Of the 5,000 to 6,000 women brought into this camp, only 200 to 300 came back." (26)

"Of 10,000 Greeks, 1,000 remained alive, and they were sent, together with 500 Jews, to Warsaw to work on fortifications. A few weeks later several hundred of them came back in miserable shape and were immediately gassed. The others died, presumably in Warsaw." (104)

"Two shipments of Czechs that arrived at the camp in March 1942 were taken to the mobile gas chambers and then burned in the ditches." (86)

"In the summer of 1942, 10,000 prisoners were delivered to the camps. Because they were Jews or political activists, they were all exterminated within a month." (121)

"When the Hungarians arrived, they were exterminated day and night for two straight months. There were between 600,000 and 700,000 of them. The five ovens were not enough. Graves had to be dug." (35)

"3,000 to 4,000 Gypsies were delivered to this camp each day. They were mostly women whose husbands were serving at the front, but there were also some children under 12 whose fathers were at the front and whose mothers worked in the factories. All of them came from tribes of Gypsies who lived on German soil." (94)

"On August 1, 1944, around 2,000 Gypsies, left over from a group of 20,000 that had already been decimated from sickness and especially brutal treatment, were exterminated." (102)

"All the Gypsies were ultimately exterminated. They were dealt with in the following manner: Some of them were sent to Auschwitz; those who remained in Birkenau were sent to the gas chamber. Then those who had been sent to Auschwitz were brought back to be gassed.

"The number of people who were selected was so high that only the number of those who remained was recorded." (35)

"At night you could see flames 30 feet high shooting out of the chimneys of the ovens." (35)

SELECTION UPON ARRIVAL

"I was very worried because my mother, who had been deported with us, had gotten separated from me upon arrival. At that time I didn't yet know what it was all about, and I asked one of the workers in the camp: 'What will happen to my mother?' The answer was: 'You won't see your mother again.'" (44)

"A friend of mine, who had traveled with her mother and who was carrying her daughter in her arms, wanted to fix her garter as we left the train, so she handed the child to her mother for a few minutes. While she was fixing her garter, both her mother and her child were swept up in the crowd and propelled down the platform, moving ever farther away from her. She wanted to run after them, but she got such a blow from the supervisor that she passed out only to wake up in the camp, where she learned the fate of her mother and her child." (10)

"From then on the only people admitted into the camp were men between 15 and 50 and women between 15 and 40 who were strong and healthy and who were not accompanied by children." (102)

"One evening at the railway overpass we happened upon a shipment of old people and children who were being taken directly to the gas chamber. This happened at the beginning of August 1942." (10)

"As each shipment arrived, selection took place. Those who were able-bodied—i.e., were strong enough to survive the exhausting work, the privation, and the abuse—were separated from the others." (23)

"Two groups were formed at the discretion of an SS guard, who pointed either to the right or to the left." (70)

"In the first group were children of both sexes under 15, men over 50, women over 40, women of any age who had a child with them, and the sick or those unable to work." (102)

"Also pregnant women were not admitted into the camp." (103)

"And while the members of the second group, the 'select,' traveled to the camp on foot, the old people, the women, the children, and the sick boarded the trucks that would take them straight to the gas chambers. Often the SS guards asked the women which of them felt bad. If one of them happened to say that she didn't feel well, she was put aboard the truck that went directly to the gas chamber." (24)

"They told those who were able go on foot: 'Don't be afraid, trucks are coming for you.'" (16)

"The SS chief physician of the camp illustrated the hypocrisy of the whole situation when, upon the arrival of one shipment, he made the following statements: 'Ladies, listen to me, your child will catch cold.' 'You ladies are ill and exhausted from such a long trip; trust your child to us.' 'You will find your child again in the children's section.'" (57)

"As a rule, Jewish children were gassed immediately upon arrival at the camp." (86)

"It could be said that in Auschwitz, for example, there were no children, for they were done away with upon arrival." (23)

"In 1944 a railway line led directly to the gas chambers. Selection took place on the train, and when it arrived, the people were taken either to the camp or to the gas chambers." (10)

"When we arrived at the camp, we climbed out of the boxcars as well as we could only to find that the train station was surrounded by Lithuanians in SS uniforms, all armed with machine guns. They immediately sealed up the cars containing the children and old people, and the train moved on." (104)

"Only a few of us made it to the camp alive." (163)

"Three-fourths of one shipment were gassed and the rest went to the work units or to the extermination compound." (93)

"For example, out of 1,200 persons in one shipment only 200 to 250 people made it to the camp; i.e., those whose death had merely been postponed. The percentage of 'provisional survivors' fluctuated, depending on the shipment, somewhere between 15 and 25 percent." (102)

"After selection, only 391 made it to the camp out of 1,300 who had departed from France; all the others were gassed." (23)

"On the 15th of April, a shipment of about 2,000 people (about 800 men, the rest women and children) arrived at the camp from Czechoslovakia. After selection, 90 percent of the prisoners were taken to a small white house just outside the camp that served in the early days as a gas chamber. There they were gassed." (76)

"Only about 100 to 150 people made it inside the camp; the rest were taken directly to the gas chamber. In was in this way that millions of people disappeared: political prisoners, Jews, Communists, as well as Russian POW's." (103)

"The gas chambers operated almost nonstop. After 1942 all Jews delivered to the camp went directly to the gas chambers. A large number of Spanish POW's who had been taken out of the stalags suffered the same fate. In less than one year, 11,000 of them were exterminated." (121)

"Of the 4,000 French prisoners who went to Sachsenhausen, only a few were allowed to remain in the camp; the rest were branded as terrorists and executed even before they were registered." (19)

"One September day we saw 5,000 men and 3,000 women go to their deaths. A large contingent of Czechs and Austrians, along with those who had been evacuated from the Polish camps at Lodz, Radom, and Theresienstadt, were liquidated by the Germans. Of the 75,000 who arrived from Theresienstadt, 60,000 were gassed." (102)

"The Russian POW's who had arrived at the camp after 1943 were taken away one night in a yellow van in which they were immediately gassed." (86)

"In 1943, a shipment of Greek Jews arrived at Birkenau. I saw two brothers of mine I had not seen in 15 years. They brought me news of my mother who, like all my relatives, had been killed. Of 1,500 Greek Jews in the camp at Jaworjno, only about 50 remained alive when the camp was evacuated on January 17, 1945." (18)

"60,000 Jews arrived from Saloniki of whom scarcely 200 survived." (12)

"In 1943, incidentally, it was Greece that supplied the most Jewish victims." (18)

"Very often whole shipments were exterminated immediately upon arrival." (100)

"After the assassination of Gestapo hangman Heydrich in Prague, thousands of Czechs were rounded up and immediately executed. At the end of that same year, in November and December, several thousand women and children of Yugoslavian partisans from Montenegro were brought to the camp." (121)

"In March 1944, a massive execution of 10,000 Czechs took place. But May 1944 was for us the moment when the fatal curve that we were on reached its zenith: Shipments of mostly Hungarian Jews followed each other without interruption. We saw up to six trains per day arrive, and this tempo continued for two and a half months. Several of us managed to count the number of boxcars (48 to 60 per train). They were all packed full. All day long, in endless rows, the condemned clogged the entrances to the gas chambers." (102)

"50 yards away from me, on the railway platform, I could see that selection was already being done, sometimes by the doctor, sometimes by his chauffeur. They sent men, women, and children to the crematory, never to be seen again. On days like this the ovens operated day and night, and the smoke from the burning flesh spread over everything. In six weeks they cremated 520,000 men, women, and children." (76)

"During the month of June 1944, 40,000 men, women, and children were sent to the gas chamber.

"Since the basic purpose of this camp was to exterminate as many people as possible as fast as possible, it was aptly called 'Extermination Camp.'" (66)

GASSING AND BURNING

"When they arrived at the place of execution, which was surrounded by a double barbed-wire fence, the men, women, and children had to take all their clothes off, after which each was given a towel and a piece of soap. Then they were led into the building until it was completely full." (104)

"On one occasion the women refused to undress. One of them, an Italian Jewish girl, lunged at one of the SS officers, snatched his revolver, and shot him dead and wounded another right there in the gas chamber." (35)

"Of the many episodes I witnessed, one especially sticks in my mind. I had been in the camp two or three weeks when a group of about 200 Belgian Israelis appeared. They were taken immediately to the gas chambers. Among them was one young Israeli girl of exceptional beauty who was holding a child of about three in her arms. The SS guard looked her over and said: 'Come with me to the barracks and I will postpone your fate a few hours.' Instead of an answer, the young woman pointed to the child in her arms. 'That's not what I have in mind,' cried the guard, and he tore the child out of the mother's arms. The child began to laugh, thinking that the officer wanted to play, and leaned forward, apparently intending to give the German a kiss. Without a moment's hesitation, the SS guard swung the child in a wide arc and smashed its head against the concrete wall. The child didn't even have time to cry out. In a rage, the young mother snatched the revolver from the holster on the German's belt and managed to shoot him and several other SS officers before they finally overpowered her and tortured her to death in the anteroom of the gas chamber." (101)

"When the chambers were full, SS executioners decided to throw the children in with the grown-ups." (57)

"In one shipment of Jewish women, a mother got separated from her seven-month-old baby just as she was about to enter the gas chamber. Noticing that the child had been left behind, an SS guard took it by one leg and smashed its head against the wall." (39)

"A section leader once made this speech to the internees who were about to be locked in the gas chamber: 'Gentlemen, because you robbed the world, you have been brought to Birkenau. Here each person must

work at his profession: doctors, engineers, lawyers, etc. So pull yourselves together, take off your clothes, and pile them up neatly so that
you can find them again on the way out. Help us to disinfect you thoroughly, for you come from countries where epidemics are rampant.
Move in closer to each other so that we don't have to repeat the process.' The prisoners obeyed. The last ones to be shoved into the chamber that time were the doctors. Before the door of the gas chamber was
closed, the section leader called to them with a diabolical grin: 'And
now you will die like cattle.'

"The established procedure for the proper utilization of the gas
chambers mandated that men and women, now naked, were to be
squeezed so tightly together they could not move. The SS men would
then seize the children by the arms and legs and smash their heads
against a rock. Their bodies would then be tossed in over the heads of
their parents and the door shut." (123)

"Oh! My God, what an apocalyptic vision: The cries of mothers
pleading for pity for their children who were either in the same chamber or an adjoining one. The children crying for their parents or for their
brothers and sisters, begging God for mercy even though they were already on the threshold of death. The shrieks, the cries of desperation,
the scratching of fingernails on the walls of these ghastly chambers—I
will never forget it." (57)

"When finally all doors had been hermetically sealed, the air was
pumped out in order to reduce the oxygen content and speed up the asphyxiation." (86)

"Through an opening in the ceiling the Germans dropped canisters into one of the wire-mesh enclosed columns in the middle of the room.
The canisters contained pellets of Zyklon B saturated in prussic acid."
(111)

"Each canister had four holes through which the gas escaped. The
wire mesh columns prevented the prisoners from getting close enough to
a canister to touch it with their hands; so the gas poured forth freely
and asphyxiated them." (86)

"Fans were set in motion that accelerated the distribution of the gas
around the room." (93)

"The building, which was several stories high, was constructed of
sturdy bricks with a cement floor and a 12-foot-deep underground vault
the entire length of the building. The main floor contained an administrative office toward the front, a closet and a washroom for the SS personnel, which lay at the other end of the building, and finally the
chamber with the ovens in the middle. Inside this chamber there were
two enclosures, both of which contained three ovens, each with its own
brick hearth. Each oven could hold three corpses for a total capacity of

18 bodies.

"The floor of each oven consisted of a simple grill by means of which the ashes were removed every day at the end of the operation. The fire came from a fire chamber which covered the back two-thirds of the floor. The flames were directed at the bodies from above by means of special devices fastened inside the fire chamber. The forward section of the underground vault contained the strangulation chamber." (106)

"At first, cremation lasted 20 to 25 minutes. In one hour 36 bodies could be cremated. Then the cremations were speeded up. Instead of burning coke, they began using a fuel called 'naphtha.' The heat was further intensified by means of a special motor for regulating the air supply. The temperature in these ovens could reached as high as 1,500 degrees centigrade." (111)

"When three bodies were burned together, naturally there was no question of separating the ashes that were not emptied anyway before each new loading, and usually not until the end of the operation." (90)

"Every oven could hold two to three people each, depending on their height and weight." (86)

"Four bodies could be accommodated at the same time if their limbs were severed. In order to get as many of them in an oven as possible, the bodies were dismembered as a matter of course. The huge ovens were made of brick and iron; they were crematories with great performance capability." (111)

"I saw nine technically perfect ovens. Up to 15 bodies could be accommodated in one single oven." (90)

"The cremations were abruptly interrupted by the arrival of American tank troops in the area, so abruptly, in fact, that the SS did not have time to 'get their act together.' Thus, the various stages of torture (the sequence of operations) were there to be thoroughly examined and understood. The bodies of that morning's victims, including 120 prisoners who had died in the camp, were still heaped on a truck in the main courtyard. And the ovens had not yet been cleaned of their grisly skeletal remains, their fragments of pelvic bone and pieces of skull." (106)

"The prisoners nearest to the wire mesh column died in six or seven minutes; those farther away succumbed in eight to twelve minutes. To ensure the success of the procedure, the chamber was not opened until 15 to 20 minutes afterward." (86)

"The observation window was reserved for the SS and the Gestapo for whom it provided lurid entertainment." (93)

"After the work was done, the door of the chamber was opened. Then a ventilator dispersed the gas, and a team, called the 'special squad,' carried the bodies away." (86)

"The dead all had terrible scratches on them. In their wild desperation and frantic battle with death, they gouged out their own eyes and lacerated their own flesh." (20)

"The bodies were intertwined with each other, so tightly were they squeezed together. It was next to impossible to untangle them, so they used a sort of rod with pincers to extricate the bodies and pull them out of the chamber. One after another the bodies were removed and taken to the elevator. Before they were loaded in, a so-called 'collection team' removed false teeth and teeth made of precious metals from their mouths, and rings from their fingers. It is hard to understand why the predatory spirit is so deeply ingrained, and yet it's true.

"There was also a team of four dental specialists whose job it was to extract gold fillings from the mouths of the dead." (93)

"From the gas chambers the bodies were taken straight to the crematory for burning." (111)

"I often saw the trucks and trailers going back and forth between the gas chamber and the crematory. On the way from the gas chamber they were loaded with bodies; on the way back they were empty." (111)

"The women's hair was also cut off before they were cremated." (86)

"The bodies were taken up by elevator to the higher floors where there were six ovens which turned 36 bodies to ashes in 20 minutes; i.e., 108 bodies per hour—2,592 in 24 hours, for they cremated without interruption." (57)

"The floor of many gas chambers contained a trapdoor which opened directly onto huge crematory ovens." (120)

"The Germans went to great lengths to make sure that this part of their activities was kept absolutely secret. The interns were never allowed to get anywhere near the chambers or the ovens. Those who were assigned to work in those facilities (transporting bodies, pulverizing bones after cremation, etc.), who made up the 'special squad,' lived apart from the others. Any contact with them was forbidden. As a way of exercising extreme caution, the personnel of the special squads was frequently 'renewed.' Thus a team of 250 Russian POW's that had only been assembled in July 1942 was totally eliminated in August and replaced by 250 Jews who were executed before the year was out." (102)

"After that the squads assigned to the crematory were made up entirely of Jews who worked under the supervision of SS men. The fact that the Jews who were sent there were not allowed to leave accounted for the frequent turnover of personnel. These prisoners lived at their workplace; they were completely separated from their comrades. The members of the special squads were well fed." (101)

"Every member of these squads received the following additional rations daily: 500 grams of bread, 60 grams of marmalade, 45 grams of butter, and 50 grams of sausage." (60)

"This work was not hard; the dead were as light as a feather." (67)

"They performed their functions for exactly 90 days. On the 91st day they were either cast alive into the ovens or gassed first. The members of these special squads had the privilege of choosing between these two methods of execution." (101)

"Between 1942 and 1944 the manpower of these special squads must have reached 800, and internees of various nationalities were assigned to them in turn (no one could escape this assignment)." (101)

"Was it possible to refuse to do this work? I think not. The following example is proof of that: In March 1944 a shipment of Jews arrived at Birkenau from German-occupied Corfu. Selection yielded 400 strong, able-bodied workers who were sent to the crematory to be shown the work they were to do. They refused and were gassed as a group." (86)

"From the entrance to the infirmary we could see that the ovens, whose doors opened every half hour to accept new loads, were no longer efficient enough. The Germans then ordered an enormous ditch to be dug and had the bottom covered with dry wood. They then stacked the bodies on this pyre and burned them." (102)

"Burning bodies on pyres was carried out in ditches 50 yards long, three or four yards wide, and of varying depths. The bottoms of these graves were covered with a layer of wood. On this layer of wood was placed a layer of bodies, and then alternate layers of wood and bodies up to the top. When the ditch was full, they poured gasoline over the pile and set fire to it. On the bottom of the grave a little canal had been dug along which human fat ran into a container at the end of the canal. The contents of this container were poured on the embers to make the fire burn faster." (86)

"By feeding them to the flames one after the other in rapid succession, they burned 10,000 to 12,000 bodies from a Hungarian shipment in a very short time." (23)

"They reached the point where they were burning up to 15,000 bodies per day. For June 27, 1944, the head Kapo of the 'special squads' reported a figure of 24,000 bodies cremated.

"In the intense fires in Krempetz Forest, more than 300,000 bodies were burned. In the fires of the camp itself, at the crematory, at least 400,000 were consumed." (111)

"In the night the spectacle was impressive. The SS came to admire it and to enjoy themselves." (101)

"The ovens operated around the clock consuming the the daily toll of dead bodies or of prisoners still breathing after a botched execution." (101)

"Frequently they ran short of gas." (123)

"Or the Germans didn't have time for gassing." (57)

"Regardless, the executions continued." (123)

"To speed things up, the Germans starting burning children and old people alive. This I can state with absolute certainty because I saw it at the place where I was." (10)

"The flames then spread across this mass of living humanity." (123)

"The victims were pitched directly into the white-hot fire." (57)

"The victims were thrown in naked and then doused with gasoline, which was then ignited." (123)

"In the camp there were patients who, when their condition worsened, were sent alive to the ovens." (24)

"The head of the crematory, a high-ranking officer, bound a Polish woman hand and foot and threw her into the oven alive." (111)

"With my own eyes I saw how the SS burned alive 14 Russian and 5 Polish officers, all in uniform." (51)

"In May 1944, 100 Jews from Athens, who unanimously refused to work in the 'special squads,' were killed on the spot; some shot, the others burned alive." (102)

"In March 1945, 500 people were killed by being thrown alive into the oven." (24)

"800 to 900 yards from the place where the ovens were, the prisoners were squeezed into little cars that ran on rails. In Auschwitz these cars had various dimensions and could hold up to 15 people. As soon as a car was loaded, it would be set in motion on an inclined plane that traveled at full speed down a corridor. At the end of the corridor there was a wall, and in the wall was the door to the oven. As soon as the car hit the wall, the door opened automatically, and the car would dip forward and pitch its cargo of living people into the oven. Right behind it came another car with another load, and so on." (101)

"It often happened that little children, still alive, were mixed in with the dead and thrown onto dump trucks." (104)

"Many eyewitness reports confirm that children were thrown alive into the ditches." (86)

"In one shipment there was a Polish Jewish woman who had a very pretty three-year-old daughter. The woman was aware of the existence of the gas chamber at Auschwitz and knew what fate awaited her. When the squad leader came past her, she begged him, since she knew she had to die, to spare her child. The squad leader flew into a rage and said: 'Damned Jew, I don't take orders from you.' He then grabbed the child by the breast and carried her to the oven while the mother ran after him screaming. He ordered the door of the oven opened and threw the child in alive." (90)

"They threw living children up to the age of ten into the ovens. Children under 90 pounds were sent automatically to the ovens." (20)

"In one shipment there were almost 400 children who were burned alive." (23)

"Many, many prisoners were burned alive." (107)

"In one single camp a million unfortunate Jews died, some of typhoid fever, some of typhus, but most were burned alive in the ovens." (121)

"After the cremation there were lots of bones, which were used to harden the earth for new road construction or else ground up and thrown in the ditches that served as latrines." (90)

"The 'Hitlerians' had the bone shards ground up into a 'special grind.' The ashes were sold to a German phosphate factory for fertilizer. The Russian Commission on War Crimes, which undertook an investigation on the very spot, uncovered agreements between the German firm in question and the camp authorities. These agreements included a clause which stipulated that the ashes delivered must be of a certain 'caliber.' The commission found in this extermination camp over 1,500 cubic yards of compost made up of manure and the ashes of burnt bodies as well as tiny slivers of human bones." (111)

"When the cremated person had a family whose address was known, the family would be sent the following letter:

> Our doctors did all in their power to save the precious life that was entrusted to them, but their efforts were in vain. Your husband (or some other relative) succumbed to pneumonia (or some other illness). After we performed the last rites for the deceased, we had his remains cremated; but we kept his ashes. If you should wish to have your relative's ashes, please remit the sum of 150 marks and we will send them to you without delay.

Upon receiving this letter, the family would rush to come up with the 150 marks. The camp authorities would then dip at random into the piles of ashes that accumulated daily, scoop up a box full, and send them to the bereaved." (101)

"The ashes the family received had nothing to do with the ashes of the deceased, but this fraud brought in huge sums of money to the camp administration." (86)

"The family could receive the ashes of just about any dead person. It so happened that both the wife and the mother of one deceased prisoner received deliveries of what were supposed to be one man's ashes.

"Once we were asked to deliver to the director of the crematory a bunch of letters received by the SS doctors in the infirmary, so we took the opportunity to open these letters in secret. They came from mothers and wives of prisoners who had died in Buchenwald asking to have wreaths laid on their graves, candles lighted, and the bill sent to them." (90)

"In addition to this systematic extermination, many deportees died of other causes every day, and you could often see mounds of corpses piled up on the ground. Sometimes they remained there until the rats ate them." (99)

"The number of dead grew steadily. In the quarantine compound there were many piles of dead bodies." (21)

"About 700 internees died per day. There were corpses that had been neither buried nor burned and since December had rotted." (48)

"There was, of course, a special detail for the collection of corpses that normally was supposed to function every morning, but it didn't get to every corner of the camp." (30)

"For disciplinary reasons, the Russian prisoners of war were often taken out of prisoner-of-war camps and brought to Auschwitz or Birkenau. One day we came upon some who were suffering appalling conditions of neglect, living in an unfinished building which afforded them almost no protection from cold and rain. They were starving in great numbers. Hundreds and thousands of their bodies had been buried in graves so shallow that a pestilential stench fouled the air. We had to dig up the bodies and bury them again." (104)

"Sometime in October or November of 1944, they ran out of coal to stoke the ovens and the corpses could not be cremated. They remained piled up near the ovens, and the methodical Germans had them stacked crosswise in neat piles of approximately 500. Thousands of putrefying bodies were massed there ready for the ovens. In March, with the first warm rays of the sun, the bodies began to reek horribly." (7)

"It took a special team with special equipment to dig a ditch big enough to bury the dead. Every day the team would pile up a daily quota of bodies at one end of the ditch, and it went on this way until all the bodies were finally buried. The number interred in this way during one month of mass burial reached about 1,200. (This information was reported by General de Lattre de Tassigny, Captain William Bullit, and an army surgeon. All these officers inspected the camp.)

"In another camp, 1,800 bodies had been gathered up and stacked like firewood in the courtyard in expectation of a new supply. To the dismay of the SS, these bodies clogged the courtyard and threatened to be a cumbersome and unpleasant obstacle. Furthermore, an anticipated drought further aggravated the situation. In general, burials were less effective than cremations and did not always conform to prescribed procedures. At any rate, something had to be done. So, a fleet of trucks and a special team of internees were assembled. The bodies were loaded onto the trucks and driven out of the camp. The special team dug a huge ditch, dumped the bodies in, filled up half the length of the grave, and covered the bodies with earth. Then the SS men killed the members of the special team with their revolvers, dumped their bodies in the other half of the grave, and covered them up with earth." (106)

"Elsewhere an oven broke down, and the Germans turned a quarry into a mass grave. The dead were tossed into the quarry, and each layer of bodies was covered with mixture of chlorine and earth." (30)

"When we arrived at Bergen-Belsen on April 11, 1945, towards 11 o'clock, we saw a horrifying spectacle such as we never could have imagined: 22,000 bodies lay there, piled up between the barracks so high that sometimes we had to climb over them. They rotted there, without being taken to the ovens or the mass graves, and every day 700 to 800 new ones arrived." (63)

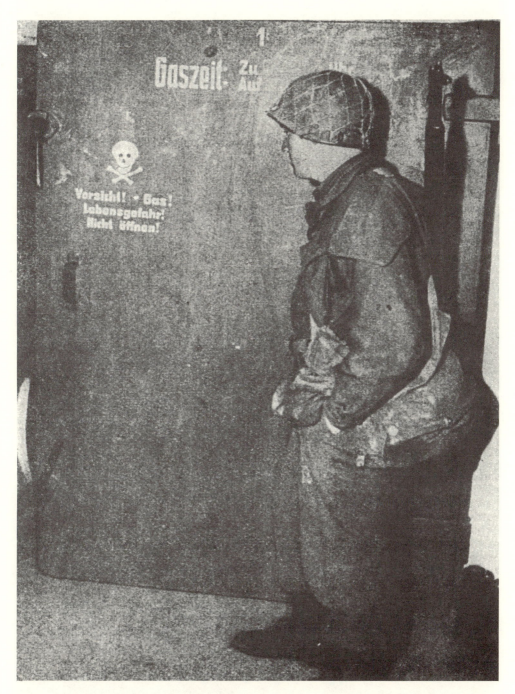

An American soldier contemplates the entrance to the control room from which cylinders of Zyklon B were released into the gas chamber

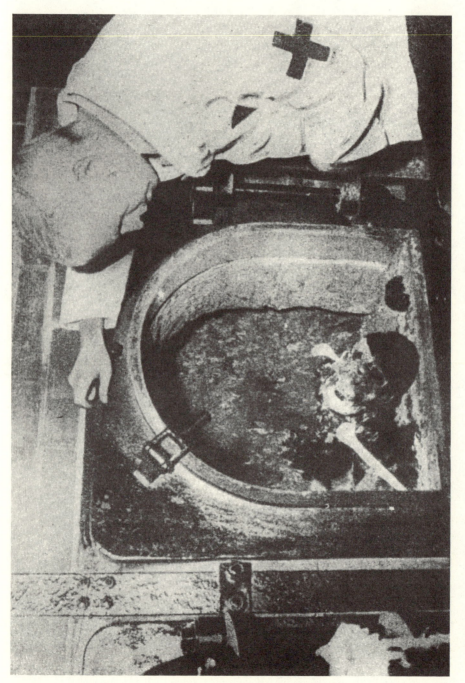

A Red Cross worker inspects the remains of a body cremated shortly before the liberators arrived

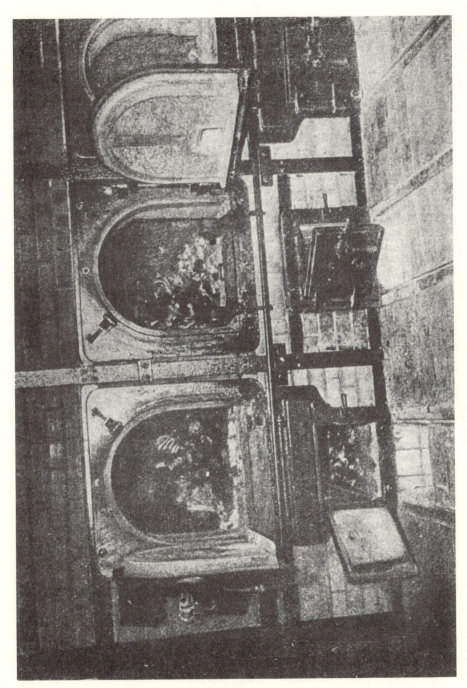

The ovens were kept busy right up to the last minute

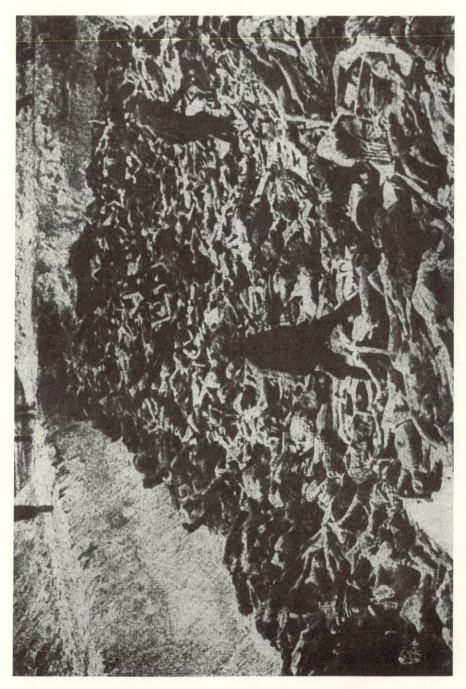

It was when mass graves like this one were still not big enough to bury all the dead that the ovens were put into operation

Chapter 12

Liberation

"Evacuation of the camp!" (39)

"The gas chambers were not bombed. The Germans blew them up."
(41)

"They used dynamite to blow up the ovens to try to keep their crimes
a secret. Only a few ruins remained of the ovens and of the place where
the Germans scattered the ashes." (107)

"They made the orderlies help with the burning of documents. I was
there during all of this, with the SS guards right behind us." (43)

"On January 18, 1945, the whole camp, i.e., the administration, the
internees, the foreign workers, etc., received the order to prepare for
evacuation." (44)

"The SS guards were furious. They gunned down all who came near
them in the courtyard. Thirty prisoners who had fled into the street
were tracked down and recaptured by the SS guards, who then returned
them to the camp. They stood the escapees against the wall and shot
all 30 of them. Then they killed another 160 persons. They drove
away and came back two hours later and shot another 100 or so prisoners. A few of the wounded begged to be killed. The guards fired three
bullets into their heads. They threw a grenade through the window of
the infirmary. We threw ourselves to the floor and no one was hurt.
The garage caught fire, but we succeed in bringing it under control before
it got out of hand." (98)

"In the afternoon the guards set fire to the barracks in which prisoners were confined, and those who tried to flee were shot." (22)

"Of the 1,200 prisoners who left Compiègne on August 17, 1944,
two-thirds died, most of them from measures taken during the course of
the evacuation of the camp on the 8th and 10th of April 1945." (69)

"Jewish deportees were the first to withdraw, followed by thieves and common criminals and, finally, political prisoners, among whom were a great many French." (84)

"The mine was evacuated on January 19, 1945, and all 2,000 of us took off on foot in the snow." (32)

"Just as we were leaving the camp, the killing began. The people who moved to the outer edges of the group were gunned down on the spot. It was the same with stragglers and the sick, anyone who could not keep up." (57)

"We marched another 15 minutes when we heard a machine gun; the Jewish women were being executed." (89)

"We covered 50 kilometers on foot without a break. Then we got a few hours rest. After that, we marched without interruption the whole night through. I will never forget it." (44)

"To make it easier for the military vehicles to get through, we were not allowed to use the main highways. We trudged down one road that was covered with two feet of snow. The marching was extremely difficult, and we sprained our ankles. Those who needed to relieve themselves had to run ahead of the group, squat by the side of the road, and be dressed again by the time the rest of the group caught up with them; otherwise they would be shot on the spot." (87)

"Thus we marched 24 hours straight. In Peiskretscham there was a big shed into which almost 1,000 people were jammed. The SS guards forced us all inside. They piled us up on top of each other, but we had no choice, for they kept firing machine guns at us. We had to lie on top of each other. Many of those who lay underneath suffocated. Nearly 100 died." (100)

"Many marched eight days and eight nights in the middle of winter, in January. Twice they were given crusts of dry bread. Other than that they received a total of two days' rations, and no water." (3)

"We marched 52 days straight. For food we got three to five potatoes. Ten times during this march we got soup and a quarter-liter of wine, and four times we got margarine." (82)

"No water. The people along the way were not allowed to give us water, so we ate snow." (39)

"Our guards let chunks of bread fall on the ground, and whoever had the misfortune to bend down and pick one up got a bullet in the head or a blow from a rifle butt. We suffered from hunger; we got to the point where we ate pieces of flesh from the buttocks and arms of recently deceased comrades. We cooked these pieces on a small fire and ate them. Whenever we stopped to rest, we threw ourselves on the cabbage patches and ate handfuls of cabbages." (98)

"Every person who collapsed on the street from exhaustion received a bullet in the head from the nearest SS guard." (78)

"Also, all those who could not keep up or tried to escape were shot." (39)

"From time to time the SS guards would decide that we were not moving ahead fast enough and, in a sort of frenzy, would fire point blank into the ranks. I was a witness to these atrocities that the SS guards committed with their guns." (87)

"I saw them kill one prisoner because he had a pair of new shoes they wanted; another, a Belgian railway employee who came from the prison at Gleiwitz, because he had had a cigarette tossed to him by a French prisoner; a third because a piece of bread had been thrown to him. Others were killed because they were lying on the left side of the barn instead of on the right as they had been ordered." (82)

"A man about 50 carried in his arms his 18 year-old son who could no longer walk. When the father was exhausted and could no longer carry his son, he laid him on the ground. The poor young man was shot on the spot by SS guards, and the father had to march on." (44)

"I was marching along with my brother and a friend of mine when an SS officer on horseback came to a halt nearby; he was accompanied by two armed soldiers. He ordered us to march on ahead. We had scarcely gone five yards into a little woods when he shot my friend in the head at close range. The bullet only grazed him, but my friend had the presence of mind to fall down and play dead. The officer then took aim at my brother and killed him. Then his revolver malfunctioned. While he was reloading it, I took off into the woods.

"I came back two hours later and found my brother's body." (68)

"Along the way, in the village of Noenschebsdorf bei Trautenau, we met up with a French worker, a POW whose papers were in order. (I saw them in his hands.) Since he wasn't able to keep up with us, he was shot by the SS guards who accompanied us. Four Rumanian POW's, who had left the hospital and joined up with us, were gunned down by the SS and and buried." (82)

"During an air raid the SS guards ran for cover in the woods but ordered the prisoners to stay where they were by the side of the road. Some of the deportees fled into the woods anyway, and the SS initiated a manhunt that resulted in quite a few deaths." (84)

"We had to dig a grave for the dead and for those prisoners who were almost dead or too exhausted to march any farther. An officer ordered those who were the weakest and could not walk to bury the bodies. Then the grave diggers themselves, about 50 in all, were shot, and some Russian POW's who had been in the camp were the ones who had to bury them. For the last stage of the journey (we had already covered 100 kilometers), we had to cover another 25 kilometers. We were nearing the battlefield. This stage was the most treacherous. The Germans were in a hurry, and we had to run. Those who could not run were shot. They killed more than a thousand people." (100)

"At one point, they crammed us into coal cars without a roof, 140 people per car. We remained in these cars for three days and three nights, standing, squeezed against each other, unable to sit or sleep. If you were totally exhausted, you leaned your head on the shoulder of your neighbor and caught a few minutes sleep. Many among us died of exhaustion." (44)

"Twice the Germans opened the cars and removed the dead. They piled them up in cars from which the living had been removed. But the trip went on, and the deaths increased. For days on end, we had to stop to gather up the bodies. After five days this task was abandoned and, to protect our own lives during the rest of the trip, we simply pitched the bodies over the side of the car." (82)

"Our shipment, which at the outset numbered 300 people, had dwindled to 32 by the time we got to Czechoslovakia on March 12, 1945." (82)

"Out of 300 in another shipment, only 15 were left. On the 3rd of May they took us and another contingent in boxcars in the direction of the American front. When we were a few kilometers away, the doors were opened so that we could relieve ourselves. I took the opportunity, along with three of my comrades, to hide out in a nearby woods. We did the right thing, for when the Americans arrived, they found somewhere between 650 and 700 bullet-riddled bodies in the cars." (89)

"1,100 women, who were in no condition to walk and therefore could not leave the camp, were locked up in two compounds, which the Germans dynamited before they left." (102)

"Of the 3,700 people we started out with, scarcely 1,500 remained. They even killed people at the camp entrance. A 14-year-old boy, a Hungarian Jew and the youngest member of the most recent shipment, fell to the ground because he could not walk any farther. He was shot by an SS guard." (100)

"About 2,000 of us remained. The SS gave us the choice of either moving on to Breslau in two hours or remaining in the camp. Those who decided to move on felt sure they were saving their own lives. There were between 200 and 300 of them. The rest of us stayed behind only because we were totally exhausted. We learned later from the Russians that those who had opted for Breslau had all been killed on orders of the SS." (87)

"Several thousand prisoners remained on the train. The SS then distributed weapons to the German prisoners who joined the SS in shooting, before our very eyes, all the prisoners who remained in the cars." (82)

"Of the 5,000 prisoners who were taken away, two-thirds died on the same day." (69)

"A shipment that had originated in Orlich arrived in Maiste, one kilometer from Gardaulgan, on April 1, 1945. The SS guards locked the prisoners in a large building and killed them the next day with grenades while a 16 year-old SS Corporal laughingly set fire to oil-soaked straw. Those who tried to flee were shot." (117)

"Of 2,500 French, over 2,000 died." (63)

"There were 5,000 of us when we left Birkenau one morning. After a trip of eight days and eight nights, the number had shrunk to about 2,500 people. The others died either from suffocation from being squeezed together or from starvation, or they were shot by the SS. The entire railroad line was strewn with bodies thrown out to make room for the living." (68)

"When we arrived on January 20, 1945, only 1,700 remained of the 4,600 people at departure. That was true for our shipment, but others suffered similar fates, although the details are sketchy." (39)

"Of the 6,000 to 7,000 prisoners on this train, only a fourth survived. Half died during the trip and the other fourth died in the infirmary a few days later." (3)

"A large shipment, whose number some put at 12,000, others at 14,000, was lured into an ambush at a place called Gleiwitz Forest in Upper Silesia. There the SS waited with machine guns and organized a mass execution. Only about 100 were able to escape this blood bath. Among those spared I saw no Frenchmen, although there were always at least a few in every shipment." (57)

"Three or four days before the arrival of the Americans there were 52,000 people in the camp. More than half were evacuated, and I learned that a very large number, if not the majority, were shot along the way." (78)

"Approximately 20,000 people left the camp. According to the results of the investigation, many were executed along the way. The exact number is hard to determine." (57)

"At Gleiwitz 12,000 prisoners were machine gunned to death in the forest. As for me, since I saw my chance to escape, I took it and got through to the Red Army." (23)

"Along the way the SS guards suddenly said to us: 'Run away!' You could hear the German machine guns firing in our direction. Already there were some dead. The guards cried: 'Go on, run, run!' We asked in which direction. The Polish Jews with their five years of experience said, 'The end has come. Pray it's over.' They knew the Germans' methods. I got away and hid myself in the woods under the snow. My friend and I remained there for three days and nights, while 20,000 prisoners were being gunned down with machine guns." (44)

"Most of the 80,000 starved and weakened prisoners the Germans forced into the streets were ultimately killed." (23)

"With the arrival of the Allies imminent, the Kommandant of the camp declared that he had orders to herd us into the barracks and set fire to them the moment the Allies began their advance. He didn't do it, initially because he thought that dysentery, typhus, hunger, and thirst would get to us first; but later because the camp was surrounded and it was too late to put this plan into effect.

"On Sunday, April 15, 1945, the English arrived. Our lives were saved, but for so many others it was too late. However, the number of dead did decline from 7,800 to 200 per day thanks to the food." (63)

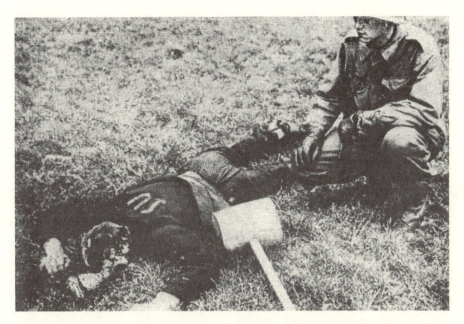

An American soldier examines the body of a Russian POW who died in the last bitter moments before liberation

The killing continued up until the last moment, even if it meant littering the camp with unburied corpses

American soldiers "liberate" a boxcar of prisoners who died on their way to a camp

More boxcars of prisoners who died on their way to a camp shortly before liberation

Rescue workers carry a starving child whose joy is clearly mixed with pain

Two prisoners greet their liberators with expressions of dazed disbelief

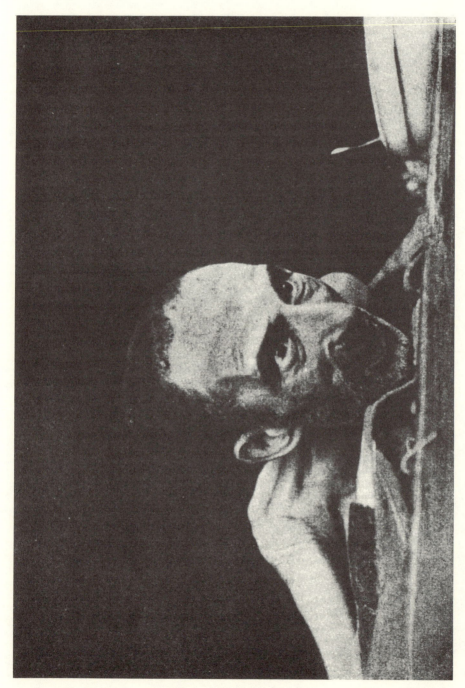

Starved, crazed, degraded—a brutalized survivor eyes both food and freedom with desperate hope

Chapter 13

Number of Dead

PERCENTAGE - BALANCE SHEET

"I can draw up the following small balance sheet: At the time I arrived, there were approximately 17,000 Russian officers and soldiers in the camp. In the course of two months, between 12,000 and 13,000 of them had disappeared." (101)

"In all about 9,000 French prisoners arrived at Mauthausen of whom about 4,400 were still alive on April 30, 1945." (118)

"The French Jews were treated no better. There was no distinction made. The Polish Jews were exterminated the moment they arrived at the camp, the French Jews a short time afterward." (94)

"Out of 80,000 Jewish deportees from Saloniki, Greece, about 100 survived. Of the 120,000 people deported from France, only about 5 percent returned. An estimate is difficult." (22)

"A comparison of the statistics on the number of Aryans and non-Aryans who died in this camp reveals that the percentage of Aryans who died was 3 to 5 percent while the percentage of non-Aryans was 95 to 96 percent. That means that if you accept a figure of 4 million killed in Auschwitz, 250,000 of them were Aryans and the rest were Jews. If you put the figure of those killed at 3 million, the number of 250,000 for the Aryans stays the same while the number of Jews changes accordingly." (86)

"The number of women who were brought to Auschwitz at this time was approximately 93,000. When these same women left Auschwitz to work at Lothringen, the number had dropped to around 12,000. This means that over 80,000 women had died in two years.

The death tally in the men's camp was even higher." (102)

"It has been proved that in the course of three months—May, June, and July 1944—the Germans cremated up to 600,000 prisoners either in ovens or on funeral pyres. During my stay, 20,000 Hungarian Jews were cremated in one day. The highest total number of cremations for one day was 36,000." (23)

"A total of 1,341,000 victims in a little less than three months." (123)

"To determine the number of dead, they requisitioned the registers of the shipments arriving at the Auschwitz railway station, which were at that time in the hands of the Russian investigative committee. In these registers the number of shipments was recorded as they passed through the station on the way to the Auschwitz camp. If you multiply the number of shipments by 1,000 (1,000 prisoners was a minimum figure for one shipment; many shipments contained up to 3,000 prisoners), you arrive at a figure of 4.5 million dead by the time that camp was liberated." (86)

"To all this mass murdering must be added the thousands upon thousands who slowly wasted away from work, torture, hunger, and sickness." (121)

"It is hard to estimate just how many prisoners actually arrived at the camp. For example, when new shipments of Russian POW's arrived, they would be given the numbers of Russians who had already died, thus making the total look much smaller than it really was." (104)

"In all, at least 7 million people were killed in Auschwitz alone. (Those who were cremated upon arrival were not entered in the register. Those who died in the camp were noted as having died by accident or from natural causes.)" (23)

"The figure of 8 million people annihilated in this camp seems in no way to be an exaggeration." (118)

"Three million for Maidanek, the camp at Lublin." (20)

"The number of surviving deportees before 1942 is extremely small, maybe one percent, maybe even less." (100)

"90 percent of our comrades died. It was a total extermination. Aryan or non-Aryan, scarcely 10 percent came back." (94)

"The number of 26 million represents approximately the total number of people, POW's and political prisoners (men, women, children, of all ages and nationalities), whom the Germans caused to die from hunger, cold, sickness, torture, medical experiments, and other means of extermination, in all the camps in Germany and in occupied territories." (118)

"Moreover, the European continent including Germany has been systematically robbed of hundreds of thousands of leading personalities of the free, democratic world." (106)

Chapter 14

Before the War

"The camp at Ravensbrück was built in 1934. It was intended for enemies of the regime. To accommodate 3,500 people, it was enlarged twice and included a total of 32 barracks.

"From 1938 on the camp was used for interning deported women." (118)

"Ravensbrück was built according to a personal plan of Himmler's." (114)

"The camp at Mauthausen was put in service in 1938 and served to intern opponents of the National Socialist regime. Ultimately, this camp was also used as an extermination camp, but on a smaller scale. Mauthausen opened in 1938 and by 1945 could report a death toll of 140,000." (11)

"The camp at Buchenwald was founded in July 1937. The first prisoners arrived there in several shipments from the camps at Sachsenhausen and Lichtenberg. They included political prisoners, criminals, and draft dodgers. During its construction, i.e., until about March 1938, people died mainly from being shot while attempting to escape, a risk they took because of the terrible living conditions in the camp. The massive arrivals in May-June 1938 of the German 'work dodgers' and Jews prompted an increase in deaths: 10 percent of the camp died between June and the end of the year.

"In 1938, after the annexation of Austria, the first foreign prisoners arrived at Buchenwald. On the pretext of trying to escape, several leading figures were taken to a quarry and shot, including Certes, son-in-law of former Minister-President Miklas; Justice Minister and Attorney General Ritterstein; Prison Warden Trummer; Head of the Secret Service and Consul, General Staidle; Major Hoffren; and the Police President of the Province of Salzburg, Bechinie.

"In December 1938, the camp Kommandant had Block 3, a special 'black barracks,' set aside. Prisoners who were confined there received only one liter of soup every third day and 25 lashes a day on the buttocks. 80 to 100 internees received this punishment; only three of them survived." (105)

"In 1937 I was in Berlin. Everyone knew what a concentration camp was and what sort of treatment the Jews and Communists confined in Dachau received. One prisoner told me that from Pastor Niemöller's cell you could hear very clearly the cries of people being tortured." (124)

Appendix

LIST OF CAMPS, COMMAND POSTS, AND PRISONS USED AS PLACES OF INCARCERATION

Incomplete identification of some internment camps reflects omissions in the original documentation due almost certainly to the unusual circumstances under which this information was gathered and processed.

Name	Location	Purpose
Aachen	Rhineland	political prisoners
Abderoda	Thuringia	women's prison/ war works
Adersbach	Erzgebirge	underground installations
Ahlbeck	Pomerania	underground workshops
Ahrensboek	Holstein	camp for Jews
Aichach	Upper Bavaria	
Aivrach		
Albala		
Algoa		camp for Jews
Allach	Upper Bavaria	political prisoners
Allendorf	East Prussia	processing camp
Allett		
Alt-Beelitz	Brandenburg	war works
Alt-Diber	Brandenburg	war works
Altkirch	Alsace	prison
Amberg	Bavaria	reprisal camp
Ampfing	Lower Bavaria	political prisoners
Amstetten	Württemberg	prison
Am Suhrskamp	Hamburg	state police prison
Andalou		
Ankenburg	Baden	war works
Annaberg	Upper Silesia	prison
Annaburg	Saxony	war works
Annen-Witten	Westphalia	work camp
Anrath	Rhineland	work camp for women

Ansbach	Franconia	camp for Jews
Anusberg	near Munich	work camp
Apfelbach		
Apolda	Thuringia	war works
Arnstadt	Thuringia	war works
Arolsen	Thuringia	
Artern	Saxony	Buchenwald Command
Arving	Rhineland	work camp
Aschenburg	Mecklenburg	camp for Jews
Aschendorf	Hanover	peat cutting
Aschendorfer Moor	Hanover	peat cutting
Aschersleben	Saxony	Malachit AG
Atlantikhaus	Berlin	Gestapo prison
Auerbach	Saxony	underground work plant
Augsburg	Bavaria	Gestapo prison
Augustow I	northeast Poland	work camp for Poles
Augustow II	northeast Poland	work camp for Poles
Aunau	near Augsburg	political prisoners
Aurich	Hanover	Neuengamme Command
Auschwitz I	Upper Silesia	political prisoners/Jews
Auschwitz II	Upper Silesia	camp for medical experiments
Auschwitz III	Upper Silesia	extermination camp
Auschwitz-Brieg	Upper Silesia	salt mines
Aussig	Czechoslovakia	
Auzun	Czechoslovakia	underground work plant
Babelsberg	near Berlin	political prisoners
Bad Berka	Thuringia	underground work plant
Bad Dürkheim	Palatinate	work camp
Bad Dürrheim	Baden	work camp
Bad Ems	Hesse-Nassau	work camp
Baden-Baden		work camp for Russians
Bad Godesberg	Rhineland	
Bad Helmstedt	Brunswick	
Bad Kreuznach	Rhineland	
Bad Liebenzell	Württemberg	prison
Bad Opersdorf	Czechoslovakia	political prisoners
Bad Salzungen	Thuringia	
Bad Schwarzbach	Lower Silesia	political prisoners
Bad Schwarzenbach	Thuringia	work camp
Bad Sulza	Thuringia	political prisoners
Bartensleben	Saxony	salt mines
Barth	Pomerania	V 1 work plant
Basel	Alsace	camp
Baumholder	Rhineland	
Bauschwitz	Upper Silesia	Auschwitz I Command
Bautzen	Saxony	political prisoners
Bayenthal	Rhineland	

Bayreuth	Upper Franconia	political prisoners
Beerfelde	near Berlin	political prisoners
Beidsburg	Bavaria	
Belgrade	Yugoslavia	work camp
Belsen	Hanover	political prisoners
Belzig	Brandenburg	munitions factory
Bendorf	Rhineland	salt mines
Bengerbrück	Rhineland	Heinkel works
Benitz	Hanover	Metallurgy AG
Benninghausen	Rhineland	
Bentkau	Lower Silesia	camp for Jews
Bentschen	western Poland	work camp
Berdingew	eastern Poland	work camp
Berensbostel	Hanover	
Berga-Elster	Saxony	work camp
Bergedorf	near Hamburg	work camp
Bergen-Belsen	Hanover	political prisoners / Jews
Bergkamen	Westphalia	mines
Bergneustadt	Rhineland	
Bergstadt	Upper Silesia	camp for Jews
Berlekau	Poland	Gestapo prison
Berlin-Albrechtstraße	Berlin	Gestapo prison
Berlin-Alexanderplatz	Berlin	police prison
Berlin-Altmoabit	Berlin	interrogation prison
Berlin-Atlantikhaus	Berlin	Gestapo prison
Berlin-Charlottenburg	Berlin	interrogation prison
Berlin-Columbushaus	Berlin	Gestapo prison
Berlin-Friedrichsfelde	Berlin	Gestapo prison
Berlin-Gestapohaus Börse	Berlin	Gestapo prison
Berlin-Kaiserdamm	Berlin	Gestapo prison
Berlin-Lehrter Straße	Berlin	Gestapo prison
Berlin-Lichtenberg	Berlin	Gestapo prison
Berlin-Lichterfelde	Berlin	interrogation prison
Berlin-Ploetzensee	Berlin	disciplinary prison
Berlin-Seidlitzstraße	Berlin	Gestapo prison
Berlin-Tegel	Berlin	disciplinary prison
Bernau	near Berlin	Gestapo prison
Bernau	Upper Bavaria	political prisoners
Berum	Hanover	peat cutting
Berum	Upper Silesia	political prisoners / Jews
Bethau	Saxony	
Beuchow	Thuringia	Buchenwald Command
Beuthen	Upper Silesia	political prisoners / Jews
Bialystock	northwest Poland	
Bielefeld	Westphalia	
Bielitz	Czechoslovakia	political prisoners / Jews
Bingen	Rhineland	camp for the infirm

Bingerbrück	Rhineland	railway prison
Birnbaum	western Poland	
Bischofskoppe	Lower Silesia	work camp for Jews
Bissingen	Bavaria	oil production works
Bitsch	Lorraine	camp
Bitterfeld	Saxony	work camp
Blaichach	Bavaria	BMW plant
Blankenau	Thuringia	
Blankenburg	Harz	aircraft plant
Blankenhain	Thuringia	
Blechhammer	Upper Silesia	camp for French prisoners
Bleicherode	Hesse	camp
Blumenau	near Mannheim	camp
Blumenthal	near Leipzig	work camp
Boberstein	Saxony	political prisoners
Bochum	Westphalia	Gestapo prison
Bocken	Rhineland	political prisoners
Boetzow	near Berlin	work camp
Bojanowo	Poland	
Bolmenen	Bavaria	Messerschmidt plant
Bonnhagen	Mecklenburg	prison
Börgermoor	Oldenburg	peat cutting
Borgo-Sandalmazzo		
Born	East Prussia	Gestapo prison
Bornim	near Potsdam	
Brandenburg		Gestapo prison
Braunsberg	East Prussia	
Braunschweig		Buchenwald Command
Braunschweig-Schandelach		industrial works
Brauweiler	Rhineland	prison
Breinke		
Bremenblumenthal	Upper Silesia	Borsig plant
Bremen-Farge		Gestapo prison
Bremen-Nißler		interrogation prison
Bremen-Ostertor		interrogation prison
Bremen-Steintor		disciplinary prison
Breslau	Silesia	camp and prison
Brieg	Silesia	camp and prison
Bromberg	Poland-West Prussia	
Brual-Rhede	Hanover	
Bruchsal	Baden	medical experiments
Brühl	Saxony	
Bruna-Worjo	western Poland	
Bruss	Poland-West Prussia	
Bruss-Konitz	Poland-West Prussia	political prisoners/Jews
Brussau	Saxony	political prisoners
Bruttig	Rhineland	camp

Brüx	Czechoslovakia	oil production
Buchau	Württemberg	
Buchenwald	Weimar	political prisoners/Jews
Buchloe	Bavaria	
Bühl	Baden	political prisoners
Bunzlau	Lower Saxony	
Burg Hoheneck	Rhineland	
Burg Hohnstein	Saxony	
Burzau	Holstein	work camp
Bussin	Pomerania	
Butzbach	Hesse	prison
Bützow-Dreibergen	Mecklenburg	prison
Bydgozcz	Poland	
Celle	Hanover	prison, camp for Jews
Cernay	Alsace	camp
Cerzandu	Poland	
Cham	Upper Bavaria	
Charbow	Pomerania	camp
Chelmno	Poland	
Chemnitz	Saxony	political prisoners/Jews
Christianstadt	Brandenburg	political prisoners/Jews
Clamenburg	East Prussia	Gestapo prison
Coburg	Franconia	political prisoners
Cochem	Rhineland	
Colditz	Saxony	war industry
Colmar	Alsace	camp
Colopiski		
Conauschigen	Alsace	
Coswig	Saxony	political prisoners
Cracovie	Poland	political prisoners/Jews
Crimmitschau	Saxony	prison
Czanew	Poland	political prisoners/Jews
Cziechanow	Poland	political prisoners/Jews
Dachau	Bavaria	political prisoners/Jews
Dalum	Hanover	peat cutting
Danzig	Poland	prison
Danzig-Langfuhr	Poland	camp
Darmstadt	Hesse	prison
Dautmergen	Württemberg	
Demblin	Poland	
Derendorf	Brandenburg	work camp
Dessau	Anhalt	Gestapo prison
Deutz	Saxony	camp for women
Deutz bei Köln	Rhineland	
Dewangen	Rhineland	
Dicharhoff	Württemberg	
Dieburg	Hesse	political prisoners

Dietz	Hesse	prison
Dietzdorf	Lower Silesia	
Dietzenbach (Hesse)	Hesse	camp
Dillenburg	Hesse	political prisoners
Ditdorf	Saxony	Krupp plant
Dobrzyn	central Poland	
Dollersheim	Hesse	
Donaueschingen	Baden	prison
Donauwörth	Bavaria	Gestapo prison
Dora	Thuringia	Buchenwald Command
Dorchutscha	Poland	political prisoners/Jews
Dornburg	Anhalt	Proedel plant
Dorndorf	Thuringia	
Dortmund	Westphalia	Gestapo prison
Dossel	Westphalia	
Dreetz-Neustadt	Brandenburg	political prisoners/Jews
Dreibergebn	Mecklenburg	prison
Drenthe-Westerbrock	Rhineland	
Dresden	Saxony	prison
Dresden-Neustadt	Saxony	munitions factory
Druderstadt	South Hanover	
Drütte	Hanover	Goering works
Duisburg	Rhineland	Gestapo prison
Düren	Rhineland	
Düsseldorf	Rhineland	Gestapo prison
Düsseldorf-Stoffel	Rhineland	camp
Dzialdowo	East Prussia	
Ebange-Florance	Lorraine	camp
Ebelsberg	upper Austria	camp
Ebensee	Poland	sterilization camp
Eberbach	Baden	prison
Eberstadt	Hesse	work camp
Eberswalde	Brandenburg	vehicle works
Edenau	East Prussia	work camp
Eger	Czechoslovakia	political prisoners
Eichtal	East Prussia	
Eiken	Hanover	political prisoners
Eilpe	Hanover	political prisoners
Eisenach	Thuringia	political prisoners
Eisenbach	Thuringia	work camp
Elbing	East Prussia	Gestapo prison
Ellrich	Thuringia	Buchenwald Command
Elrach	Rhineland	fortifications
Elsig	Thuringia	aircraft plant
Elsing		Buchenwald Command
Emden	Hanover	peat cutting
Ems	Hanover	peat cutting

Emsland	Hanover	peat cutting
Ensisheim	Elsaß	prison
Epersheim	Hesse-Nassau	
Eppen	Rhineland	work camp
Erbruch	Brunswick	Goering works
Erfurt	Saxony	women's work camp
Erla-Leipzig	Saxony	
Erlau	Lower Silesia	
Eschershausen	Thuringia	
Essen	Rhineland	Gestapo prison
Esterwegen	Hanover	peat cutting
Ettersburg	Thuringia	Buchenwald Command
Eutin	Holstein	camp
Everstadt	Oldenburg	peat cutting
Falbrik	Poland	transit camp for Jews
Falkenau	Saxony	prison
Falkenau-Swodau	Saxony	political prisoners
Falkenheim	Brandenburg	camp
Falkensee	near Berlin	camp
Fallersleben	Hanover	Volkswagen plant
Fallingbostel	Hanover	political prisoners
Farge	Bremen	disciplinary camp
Fechenbach	Bavaria	disciplinary camp
Federnbach	Hesse-Nassau	
Feldafing	Bavaria	prison
Festung-Ankhaus	Pomerania	prison
Fichtelberg	Saxony	underground plant
Fingerlitten	Bavaria	disciplinary camp
Firnbein	near Mannheim	women's prison
Fischen	Bavaria	prison
Flehingen	Baden	prison
Flensburg	Schleswig	prison
Flöha	Saxony	aircraft plant
Florisdorf	near Vienna	Heinkel plant
Flossenburg	Bavaria	metal works
Flossenburg	Bavaria	transit camp
Flossenburg-Pilsen	Bavaria	women's camp
Flossenburg-Weiden	Bavaria	men's camp
Fochenheim	Hesse-Nassau	prison
Frais-Mauee		underground construction
Frankenstein	Lower Silesia	prison
Frankental	Upper Silesia	prison
Frankenthal	Palatinate	Gestapo prison
Frankfurt am Main	Hesse	Gestapo prison
Frankfurt an der Oder	Brandenburg	prison
Frankfurt-Preungesheim		disciplinary camp
Freiburg	Baden	Gestapo prison

Freistatt	Hanover	prison
Freudenstadt	Baden	Gestapo prison
Friedrichshafen	Württemberg	camp
Frohnau	near Berlin	Gestapo prison
Fromen	near Stuttgart	prison
Frysztat	southwest Poland	work camp
Fuhlsbüttel	near Hamburg	disciplinary prison
Fürstenberg	Brandenburg	political prisoners
Fürstenwald	Hesse-Nassau	transit camp
Fürth	Bavaria	prison
Fußbach	Baden	disciplinary prison
Füssen-Plansee	Tyrol	camp
Gaggenau	Baden	political prisoners
Ganacker	Bavaria	prison
Gandersheim	south Hanover	Buchenwald Command
Gazelle	south Poland	salt mines
Genshagen	near Berlin	Daimler-Benz plant
Germersheim	Palatinate	camp
Gerolstein	Rhineland	political prisoners
Gersheim	Palatinate	political prisoners
Ginsheim	Hesse	prison
Glasch	Oldenburg	peat cutting
Glasmoor	Oldenburg	peat cutting
Glatz	Silesia	political prisoners/Jews
Gleiwitz	Upper Silesia	political prisoners/Jews
Glücksstadt	Schleswig-Holstein	prison
Gmünd	Württemberg	prison and camp
Gocolin	Upper Silesia	camp for Jews
Godesberg	Rhineland	Gestapo prison
Golleschau	Saxony	prison
Gollnow	Pomerania	prison
Golojow	Poland	cement works
Gommern	Saxony	prison
Gorczyn I	Poland	camp for Poles
Gorczyn II	Poland	camp for Poles
Görlitz	Silesia	prison
Gortau	Saxony	prison
Gorzice	Poland	prison
Gosen	Brandenburg	disciplinary camp
Gotenhafen	near Danzig	Neuengamme Command
Gotha	Thuringia	prison
Göttendorf	Thuringia	prison
Gotteszell	Lower Bavaria	prison
Graeben	Hanover	political prisoners
Gräfenhainichen	Saxony	prison
Grajewo	Poland	transit camp for Jews
Graudenz	East Prussia	prison

Grauwinkel	Saxony	underground construction
Graz	Austria	aircraft plant
Graz-Aflenz	Austria	underground construction
Graz-Leibnitz	Austria	underground construction
Greifswald	Pomerania	disciplinary camp
Greiz	Thuringia	textile factory
Griebo	Saxony	camp
Griesheimer Sand	Hesse	disciplinary camp
Grimma	Saxony	prison
Großhennersdorf	Saxony	camp for Alsatians
Groß-Rosen	Hanover	political prisoners
Groß-Strehlitz	Upper Silesia	political prisoners/Jews
Grottau	Saxony	textile works
Grundhaus	East Prussia	camp
Grünhainichen	Saxony	prison
Grussen	Silesia	political prisoners
Güsen	Brandenburg	labor camp
Güsen	Upper Austria	Mauthausen Command
Güsten	Hanover	prison
Gustloffwerke	near Weimar	underground construction
Gutach	Baden	labor camp
Gutsch	East Prussia	political prisoners
Guttowitz	East Prussia	political prisoners/Jews
Hagen	Westphalia	Gestapo prison
Hagenau	Alsace	camp
Halberstadt	Saxony	aircraft plant
Halle	Saxony	women's prison
Hallendorf	Brunswick	camp
Hamburg-Altona	Hamburg	interrogation prison
Hamburg- Am Suhrenkamp	Hamburg	Gestapo prison
Hamburg-Damtor	Hamburg	interrogation prison
Hamburg-Fischbeck	Hamburg	Gestapo prison
Hamburg-Fuhlsbüttel	Hamburg	disciplinary prison
Hamburg-Holstengleis	Hamburg	Gestapo prison
Hamburg-Neuengamme	Hamburg	political prisoners
Hamburg-Schumeckstraße	Hamburg	Gestapo prison
Hamm	Westphalia	Gestapo prison
Hammersleben	Saxony	Malachit AG
Hammerstein	Poland-West Prussia	camp
Hanau	Hesse	Gestapo prison
Hannberg	Bavaria	transit camp for Jews
Hannover	Hanover	interrogation prison
Hannover-Limmer	Hanover	Gestapo prison
Hannover-Stonnen	Hanover	disciplinary camp
Happurg	Middle Franconia	camp
Harpstedt	Hanover	camp

Harzungen	Hanover	underground construction
Haselhorst	near Berlin	aircraft plant
Haslach	Baden	disciplinary camp
Hasselt	Rhineland	political prisoners
Hasserode	Saxony	varnish works
Haßloch	Lower Franconia	camp for Jewish women
Hattingen	Rhineland	Gestapo prison
Haunstetten	Bavaria	political prisoners
Hecht		
Hedersheim	Lower Franconia	political prisoners
Heide	Holstein	prison
Heidelsheim	Baden	camp
Heilbronn	Württemberg	Gestapo prison
Heilsberg	East Prussia	camp
Heinewalde	Saxony	
Heinrich St.	Bavaria	camp
Heinsburg	Saxony	camp
Hela	Danzig	underground construction
Helbra	Saxony	prison
Helenow	Poland	camp
Helfingen	Lower Bavaria	camp
Helmstedt	Brunswick	aircraft plant
Henschelwerke	Kassel	locomotive works
Herbestal	Rhineland	camp
Hermeskeil	Rhineland	prison
Hersbruck	Middle Franconia	labor camp
Herta	Rügen (Pomerania)	underground works
Herzingen	Bavaria	camp for medical experiments
Herzogenburg	Lower Austria	political prisoners
Hettstedt	Hanover	political prisoners
Heuberg	Württemberg	disciplinary camp
Heydebreck	Upper Silesia	political prisoners
Hinzerath	Rhineland	war works
Hirschberg	Silesia	prison
Hochpils	East Prussia	Gestapo prison
Hoevelhof	Westphalia	political prisoners
Hof	Upper Franconia	Gestapo prison
Hohen-Asperg	Württemberg	maximum security prison
Hohenbrück	Pomerania	labor camp
Hohensalza	Poland	
Hohenstein	East Prussia	labor command
Holbeckshof	Rhineland	
Holleischen	Czechoslovakia	munitions factory
Holleschau	Lower Austria	
Holweide	Rhineland	camp for the infirm
Holzen	Hanover	excavations
Homburg v.d.H.	Hesse	Gestapo prison

Hondwitz	Upper Silesia	camp for Jews
Hradisko	Czechoslovakia	political prisoners
Hütten	near Hamburg	labor camp
Huy	Saxony	political prisoners
Imperia	Austria	prison
Innsbruck	Tirol	camp
Jablonow	northwest Poland	
Janina	Poland	coal mines
Jauer	Lower Silesia	political prisoners
Jawischowitz	Poland	coal mines
Jaworino	Poland	coal mines
Jaworowo	Poland	coal mines
Jaworzina	Poland	camp for Jews
Jaworzlobelzec	Poland	political prisoners
Jaworzlow	Poland	coal mines
Jedlice	Czechoslovakia	political prisoners
Jena	Thuringia	Gestapo prison
Johannesberg	Emsland	labor camp for the infirm
Johannesdorf	Silesia	
Johanngeorgenstadt	Saxony	peat cutting
Jülich	Rhineland	camp
Jüterbog	Brandenburg	underground construction
Kaematen	Württemberg	prison
Kaismain	Bavaria	
Kalkar	Rhineland	
Kalkau	Silesia	
Kalsheim	Bavaria	
Kaltenkirchen	Holstein	camp
Kamenz	Silesia	political prisoners
Kamp	Rhineland	steel works
Karlsruhe	Baden	Gestapo prison
Karpfen	Czechoslovakia	
Kasgel b. Melsungen	Thuringia	war works
Kassel	Hesse-Nassau	Buchenwald isolation camp
Kattowitz	Upper Silesia	disciplinary camp
Kaufbeuren	Bavaria	war works
Kaufering	Bavaria	dynamite factory (Jews)
Kehl	Baden	Gestapo prison
Kelbra	Saxony	
Kemauthen	Bavaria	underground construction
Kempten	Bavaria	
Kerpen	Rhineland	
Kiel	Holstein	Gestapo prison
Kislau	Baden	prison
Kisselring-Leitmeritz	Czechoslovakia	underground works
Kittlitztreben	Silesia	
Klagenfurt	Austria	camp

Kleingladbach	Rhineland	
Klinker I	Saxony	V 1 works
Klinker II	Saxony	grenade factory
Koblenz	Rhineland	political prisoners (women)
Koblenz Karmeliter	Rhineland	
Koblenz Kartause	Rhineland	
Kochendorf	Baden	salt mines
Koechen		
Koethen	Anhalt	work camp
Koffing	Bavaria	underground labor (women)
Kola	Rhineland	
Kolmar	Alsace	
Köln	Rhineland	prison and camp
Köln-Deutz	Rhineland	IG Farben
Komotau	Czechoslovakia	political prisoners
Königsberg	East Prussia	Gestapo prison
Königshütte	Upper Silesia	
Königstein	Saxony	fortified prison
Königswusterhausen	Brandenburg	
Konitz	Poland, West Prussia	camp
Konradstein		
Konstantinow	central Poland	
Konstanz	Baden	prison
Kosel	Silesia	
Kothen	Bavaria	
Kottbus	Brandenburg	Gestapo prison
Kottern	Upper Bavaria	
Kracowinkel	Poland	tunnel construction
Krakau	Poland	
Kratzau	Austria	
Krefeld	Rhineland	
Kreuznach	Rhineland	prison
Krispl	Salzburg	
Krollista Huta		
Kuhberg	Thuringia	
Küstrin	Brandenburg	political prisoners
Kyffhäuser	Thuringia	camp
Labiau	East Prussia	
Labroque	Alsace	camp
Lademond-Husum	Holstein	coastal fortifications
Lager Nr. 21	Emsland	peat cutting
Lager Peterminschule	Constance	
Lahde	Hanover	camp
Landau	Palatinate	prison
Landsberg/Lech	Bavaria	fortified prison
Langelsheim	Brunswick	tunnel construction
Langen	Hesse	work camp

Langenbielau	Silesia	aircraft plant
Langendorf	Silesia	forest labor
Langenfeld	Thuringia	underground aircraft plant
Langenlütjen	near Bremen	political prisoners
Langensalza	Saxony	
Langern-Ravensbrück	Mecklenburg	camp for women
Langfurth	Bavaria	
Lanzendorf	Austria	transit camp
Lathen/Ems	Hanover	peat cutting
Lauffen	Württemberg	
Laura/Saalfeld	Thuringia	underground works
Lavorchond	Upper Silesia	coal mines
Lazy	Czechoslovakia	
Leau	Anhalt	
Lehe	Hanover	
Leibnitz-Aflen	Austria	
Leinbach	Saxony	political prisoners
Leipzig-Schönefeld	Saxony	ordinance works
Lengerich	Westphalia	underground aircraft plant
Leonberg	Württemberg	Malachit AG, salt mines
Leopoldshall	Saxony	
Lepschadt		camp for political DP's
Leubel-Paß	Silesia	tunnel construction
Leuforta		
Leuna	Saxony	fertilizer works
Lichtenau	Hesse	
Lichtenburg	Saxony	political prisoners
Liebau	Silesia	preventive detention
Liebenau	Hanover	
Liebenau	Württemberg	
Liepowa	Poland	political prisoners
Limburg	Bavaria	camp
Limmer	Hanover	
Lindenburg	Upper Silesia	Gestapo prison
Linsdorf	Upper Silesia	
Linz	Austria	Hermann Göring Works
Linz I	Austria	underground works
Linz II	Austria	political prisoners
Lippspringe	Hanover	camp
Lippstadt		Buchenwald disciplinary
Litzmannstadt	Poland	
Lobhof		
Lochmühle	Silesia	
Lodz I	Poland	
Lodz II	Poland	
Lodz III	Poland	
Lodz IV	Poland	

Lodz V	Poland	
Lodz VI	Poland	
Lorhof	Bavaria	political prisoners/Jews
Lübben	Brandenburg	
Lübeck-Lauerfohr	Holstein	political prisoners (women)
Lübeck-Marliring	Holstein	political prisoners (men)
Lublin-Maidanek	Poland	political prisoners/Jews
Luckau	Brandenburg	prison
Ludwigsburg	Württemberg	prison
Ludwigsdorf		transit camp for Jews
Ludwigsfeld	Bavaria	
Ludwigshafen	Palatinate	political prisoners
Ludwigslust	Mecklenburg	prison
Lukow	Poland	political prisoners/Jews
Lungwitz	Saxony	branch of Mauthausen
Luthingshausen	Hesse	political prisoners
Lützendorf	Thuringia	
Lyska	Poland	
Mackenrode	Saxony	disciplinary center
Magdeburg	Saxony	political prisoners/fortress
Maidanek	Poland	political prisoners/Jews
Mainz	Hesse	prison
Mannheim	Baden	Gestapo prison
Maret	Austria	political prisoners
Marienburg	East Prussia	fortified prison
Marienthal		underground V 1 works
Markirch-St. Marie	Alsace	tunnel construction
Markleeberg	near Leipzig	camp for French saboteurs
Matzkau	East Prussia	
Maulburg	Baden	
Mauthausen	Austria	political prisoners
Mayen	Rhineland	camp
Mechtal	Silesia	political prisoners
Meerane	Saxony	prison
Meiningen	Thuringia	prison
Meinsdorf		
Melk	Austria	Gestapo prison
Melk-Ebensee	Austria	camp, underground factory
Melsin	Pomerania	
Melsungen	Thuringia	
Merken	Rhineland	Gestapo prison
Merkendorf		
Merlenbach	Lorraine	camp
Mersin	Pomerania	excavations
Merzbach	Rhineland	
Meschede	Westphalia	political prisoners
Metz	Lorraine	prison and camp

Meuselwitz	Saxony	
Micling	Poland	
Midzychod	Poland	
Minden	Hanover	political prisoners
Misburg	Hanover	
Mittelgladbach	Rhineland	camp
Mittenbach	Rhineland	
Mohringen	Hanover	
Moll	Silesia	cement factory
Monowitz (Auschwitz III)	Silesia	political prisoners/Jews
Monterberg	Silesia	
Moorexpreß	Hanover	discipline center
Moorhausen	Hanover	camp for the infirm
Moosbierbaum		center for synthetic gas
Morzach	Bavaria	
Mosbach	Baden	political prisoners
Muerau		political prisoners
Mühldorf	Bavaria	political prisoners
Mühlhausen	Thuringia	political prisoners
Mühlheim	Rhineland	
München-Alaniheim	Bavaria	political prisoners/Jews
München-Stadelheim	Bavaria	Gestapo prison
Munderkingen	Württemberg	prison
Münster	Westphalia	political prisoners
Murnau	Bavaria	camp
Myslowitz	Poland	political prisoners/Jews
Nackel	Silesia	
Nandlstadt	Bavaria	
Nasilak	north Poland	
Natzweiler	Alsace	branch of Schirmeck camp
Naumburg	Saxony	prison
Naundorf	Austria	political prisoners
Neckarelz	Baden	political prisoners
Neckargerach	Baden	political prisoners
Neersen	Hanover	political prisoners/Jews
Neersen	Rhineland	political prisoners
Neisse	Silesia	political prisoners/Jews
Nestamitz		camp
Nestomitz		
Neuberum	Brandenburg	
Neubrandenburg	Mecklenburg	political prisoners
Neubrenne	Mecklenburg	branch of Ravensbrück
Neudorf		war works
Neuen-Bremme	Saar	political prisoners
Neuendorf	Brandenburg	political prisoners
Neuenfingen	Württemberg	
Neuengamme	Hamburg	political prisoners

Neumarkt	Bavaria	political prisoners
Neumarkt-St. Veit		
Neumünster	Holstein	political prisoners
Neuoffingen	Bavaria	political prisoners
Neusatz	Baden	political prisoners
Neustadt	Upper Palatinate	excavation (women)
Neusustrum	Hanover	peat cutting
Nieborowitz	Silesia	
Niederhagen	Pomerania	
Niederorschel	Saxony	
Niederraden	Rhineland	camp
Niederroden	Baden	work camp
Niederroden/Rodgau	Hesse	political prisoners
Niedersachswerfen	Hanover	political prisoners
Niederzwehren	Hesse-Nassau	prison
Nordhausen	Thuringia	disciplinary camp
Nürnberg	Bavaria	Gestapo prison
Obergleen	Hesse	
Oberlangen	Hanover	
Oberlangen/Ems	Hanover	peat cutting
Oberlangenau	Silesia	political prisoners
Oberlangenbielau	Silesia	political prisoners
Oberlanzendorf	Austria	
Oberndorf/Neckar	Württemberg	prison
Oberuhldingen	Baden	political prisoners
Oberwitz	Silesia	camp
Obra	western Poland	
Ochtumsand	Bremen	ship serving as a camp
Oderberg	Brandenburg	political prisoners
Oderzleen	Upper Silesia	camp
Oels	Silesia	camp
Offenburg	Baden	Gestapo prison
Ohrdurf	Thuringia	Buchenwald Command
Olbernhau	Saxony	transit camp
Oldenburg	Oldenburg	prison
Opopeln	near Berlin	oldest concentration camp
Oranienburg		
Oriburg	Saxony	prison
Orlamünde	Thuringia	camp
Ortenstein	Westphalia	prison
Osnabrück	Mecklenburg	camp
Osterhagen	south Hanover	political prisoners
Osterode	Saxony	labor camp
Osterstein	Hesse	
Osthofen	western Poland	labor camp
Ostrowo	Silesia	transit camp
Otmachau	Bavaria	prison

Ottobrunn	Bavaria	peat processing plant
Ougard	Hanover	peat cutting
Ovelhoff	central Poland	labor camp
Pabilnice	Hanover	political prisoners
Papenburger Group	Bavaria	political prisoners
Passau	Pomerania	torpedo works
Peenemünde	Saxony	prison
Pegau	Upper Silesia	political prisoners
Peiskretscham	Austria	labor camp
Petau	Steiermark	labor camp
Pettau	Bavaria	political prisoners
Pfersee	Bavaria	labor camp
Pipping	Lower Bavaria	political prisoners
Pitzling	Saxony	tunnel construction
Plauen	Mecklenburg	camp
Pleß	western Poland	labor camp
Pleszew	Silesia	salt mines
Pletz	Upper Silesia	political prisoners
Plomnitz	Anhalt	Junker plant
Plomnitz-Leau	north Poland	work camp
Plonsk	Poland	camp
Pobianize	Saxony	prison
Polatowo	central Poland	political prisoners/Jews
Polens	Poland/West Prussia	camp
Poniatowo	Westphalia	labor camp
Porta	western Poland	Gestapo prison
Posen	Poland	political prisoners/Jews
Posen-Stadion	Brandenburg	Gestapo prison
Potsdam	Brandenburg	political prisoners
Potsdam	western Poland	labor camp
Potuliz		highway construction
Povchen-Attnach	Czechoslovakia	political prisoners/Jews
Prag	East Prussia	
Prawinischki	Pomerania	labor camp
Preungesheim	Upper Austria	Mauthausen Command
Prym	Baden	prison
Puck	Litauen	labor camp
Pudy	Hesse	political prisoners
Pusyko	East Prussia	prison
Queuleu	Rhineland	prison
Rabstein	northwest Poland	prison
Radinkendorf		railway bridge construction
Radogosetsch	southwest Poland	labor camp
Raging	Saxony	prison
Raguhn	France	fortifications labor
Raming	Poland	labor camp
Rammin	Brandenburg	political prisoners

Rastatt	Brandenburg	political prisoners
Rathenow	Anhalt	aircraft plant
Ratibor	Upper Silesia	political prisoners
Ravaruska	Poland	political prisoners/Jews
Ravensbrück	Brandenburg	infamous camp for women
Ravensbrück-Kommando	Saxony	political prisoners/Jews
Ravensburg	Württemberg	political prisoners
Rebstock		
Recklingen	Saxony	airfield construction
Recklinghausen	Westphalia	political prisoners
Redel	Pomerania	camp
Redelzipf	Austria	war works
Regensburg	Lower Bavaria	political prisoners
Reh	Westphalia	salt mines
Reibnitz	Lower Silesia	labor camp
Reichenbach	Saxony	Gestapo prison
Reichenberg	East Prussia	prison
Reichling	Bavaria	munitions factory
Reil	Moselland	prison
Rellas		
Remscheid	Rhineland	Gestapo prison
Remschels	Austria	
Remsdorf		synthetic oil refinery
Rendsburg	Schleswig	political prisoners
Repnik	Lower Silesia	camp
Reutte	Hanover	political prisoners
Reval	Livonia	camp
Rheinbach	Rhineland	political prisoners
Rickling	Holstein	excavations
Rippin	north Poland	
Rischling		
Rochenburg	Silesia	camp
Röchling	Saar	steel works
Rollwald	Thuringia	Buchenwald Command
Römlitstadt		labor camp
Ronsee		
Rosendorf	Brandenburg	synthetic oil refinery
Roßlau	Anhalt	Junker plant
Rotesbor	East Prussia	political prisoners
Rothau	Alsace	branch of Schirmeck
Rothenburg/Neckar	Württemberg	political prisoners
Rottleberode	Saxony	war industry
Rottweil	Württemberg	labor camp
Rüdesheim	Hesse	prison
Rumburg	Saxony	prison
Rybnik	Silesia	prison
Rybniol	southwest Poland	political prisoners

Rydultau	Poland	coal mines
Saal-Donau	Austria	
Saarbrücken	Saar	Gestapo prison
Saarlautern	Saar	
Sachsenburg	Saxony	
Sachsenhausen	Brandenburg	political prisoners
Sachsenwerke		
Sagan	Silesia	prison
St. Aegidien	Austria	Mauthausen Command
St. Georgen	Baden	political prisoners
St. Ingbert	Moselland	
St. Poelten	Austria	political prisoners
Sakrau	Silesia	
Salzgitter	Hanover	political prisoners
Salzwedel	Saxony	
Sandbostel	Hanover	disciplinary camp
Sandhagen	Mecklenburg	labor camp
Sangerhausen	Thuringia	political prisoners
Sasselt	Mecklenburg	Ravensbrück Command
Saurerwerke		
Sazerdorf		
Schakenwerke		
Schandelbach	Brunswick	camp
Schaubitz	Saxony	mines
Schechat		
Schelkingen	Bavaria	political prisoners
Scherfeld		
Scherzingen	Baden	oil drilling
Scheveningen	Holland	camp
Schimitz	Bavaria	
Schirmeck-Natzweiler	Alsace	camp for women
Schirmeck-Vorbruck	Alsace	French political prisoners
Schlackenwerth	Czechoslovakia	political prisoners
Schlagenwald	Saxony	camp
Schleusingen	Thuringia	political prisoners
Schlieben	Saxony	war industry
Schlieben-Halle	Saxony	Buchenwald Command
Schloysthe		
Schneidemühl	Pomerania	
Schocken	East Prussia	political prisoners
Scholien	Hanover	political prisoners
Schomberg	Silesia	
Schönebeck	Saxony	Junker Works
Schönefeld	near Berlin	Henschel Works
Schönfeld		
Schöningen	Hanover	
Schönlinde	East Prussia	

Schönweide	Schleswig	
Schorin	Pomerania	camp
Schulp	Holstein	
Schurtingen		
Schwaben		camp for women
Schwabmünchen	Bavaria	camp for Jews
Schwaningen	Baden	
Schwarzach	Baden	SS compulsory training camp
Schwarzheide	Brandenburg	camp for Czech Jews
Schweidnitz	Silesia	Gestapo prison
Schwenningen	Württemberg	political prisoners
Schwerin	Mecklenburg	political prisoners
Schwerte	Westphalia	war works
Schwetz	Polish West Prussia	
Schwetzing	Mecklenburg	labor camp
Schwetzingen	Baden	camp
Schwetzy		
Semmering	Austria	prison
Senftenberg	Brandenburg	lignite mines
Sennelager	Alsace	political prisoners
Sennheim	Alsace	political prisoners
Sensen	East Prussia	transit camp
Serpeck		
Sicholberg	north Poland	camp
Sickingen	Hohenzollern	important war industry
Siegburg	Rhineland	mine defusing / fortress
Siemenswerke	Berlin	prison, munitions factory
Sigmaringen	Hohenzollern	political prisoners
Singen	Baden	prison
Sinsheim	Baden	prison
Sochen		
Soldau	northwest Poland	
Soldin	Brandenburg	camp
Sonneberg	Thuringia	camp
Sonnenburg	Brandenburg	prison
Sorau	Brandenburg	prison
Sosnowitz	Poland	
Speerwerke	Upper Silesia	metal recycling
Spergau	Saxony	disciplinary camp
Staab	Bavaria	political prisoners
Stackhausen	Thuringia	camp for deported women
Stadelheim	near Munich	prison
Stadtilm	Thuringia	camp for "the dishonorable"
Stadtroda	Thuringia	political prisoners
Stan-Krems		fortifications construction
Stargard	Pomerania	
Staßfurt	Saxony	salt mines

Stefanskirchen	Bavaria	
Steinthor	Vienna	interrogation prison
Stettin	Pomerania	prison and shipyard
Steyr	Austria	political prisoners
Stocken	Württemberg	
Stoffeln	Austria	
Strakonitz	Czechoslovakia	
Stralsund	Pomerania	prison
Straphkolow		
Strasburg	Brandenburg	prison
Straßbourg	Alsace	prison
Straubing	Bavaria	political prisoners
Straußberg	Brandenburg	political prisoners
Strelitz	Mecklenburg	
Striegau	Silesia	political prisoners
Struthof	Alsace	political prisoners
Stuhm	East Prussia	political prisoners/Jews
Stuthof	East Prussia	political prisoners
Sulz		
Sulz/Neckar	Württemberg	
Sulzbach	Baden	political prisoners/Jews
Sustrum	Hanover	political prisoners/Jews
Swientochlowitz	Poland	political prisoners/Jews
Swierczyn	Poland	labor camp for Poles
Swodau	Poland	political prisoners/Jews
Swoentoslaw	Poland	labor camp for Poles
Tallinn	Estonia	labor camp
Tannenwald	Thuringia	labor camp
Tarnowitz	Upper Silesia	women's camp
Taucha	Saxony	
Taura	Saxony	labor camp
Teltow	Brandenburg	political prisoners/Jews
Teplitz	Czechoslovakia	
Teresina		
Thale/Harz	Saxony	camp
Theresienstadt	Czechoslovakia	camp for Jewish women
Thorin/Forum	northwest Poland	camp printing press
Thorin/Forum II	northwest Poland	
Thourmalin		underground construction
Thurath		fortifications
Tolkemit	East Prussia	
Tomaszow	Poland	women's labor camp
Tomerdorf	near Rothenburg	political prisoners/Jews
Tonndorf	Thuringia	
Torgau/Buchenwald	Saxony	munitions factory
Tratenau	Czechoslovakia	labor camp
Travinka	Bosnia	political prisoners/Jews

Travniki	Poland	
Treblinka	Upper Silesia	political prisoners
Treis	Moselland	underground works
Treskau	Poland	
Trier	Rhineland	Gestapo prison
Trigenhain		
Troglitz	Saxony	Brabag plant
Troglitz-Seitz		
Troisdorf	Rhineland	IG Farben dynamite factory
Tronowitz	Poland	political prisoners/Jews
Troppau	Czechoslovakia	political prisoners/Jews
Trzebinia	Poland	
Tschakow	Upper Silesia	
Tübingen	Württemberg	prison
Türkheim	Württemberg	
Tutzing	Bavaria	labor camp
Ulm/Donau	Württemberg	prison
Unstadt	Baden	
Unterlüß	Hanover	
Untermansfeld	Saxony	mines
Untermansfeld	Thuringia	mines
Usedom	Pomerania	torpedo works
Vaihingen/Fildern	Württemberg	political prisoners
Valluhn	Hanover	
Varel	Oldenburg	prison
Vastorf	Hanover	
Vechta	Oldenburg	prison
Veddel	near Hamburg	
Venningen	Palatinate	
Verles		excavation
Verssen	Hanover	
Vilklingen	Baden	prison
Vöcklabruck	Austria	prison
Vogoli		
Vohenstrauß	Bavaria	camp
Vorbruck/Schirmeck	Alsace	camp
Vronisberg	East Prussia	political prisoners/Jews
Wadowice	Poland	political prisoners/Jews
Wagram	Austria	
Walbeck		salt mines
Walchum	Hanover	camp
Waldau		
Waldenburg	Silesia	political prisoners/Jews
Waldheim	Saxony	women's prison
Waldshut	Baden	prison
Walfen		
Walkenried	Hanover	

Walkenstest		
Walser		
Walsheim		prison, bomb defusing
Walsum	Rhineland	camp
Waltersdorf	Silesia	political prisoners
Wandsleben	Saxony	salt mines
Wanne/Eikel	Westphalia	war industry
Warschau (Warsaw)	Poland	labor camp (cleanup detail)
Wartenburg	East Prussia	political prisoners
Wartha-Breslau	Silesia	prison
Wasserburg	Bavaria	
Watenstedt	Brunswick	special camp 21
Wattenscheid	Westphalia	
Weferlingen	Saxony	
Weimar	Thuringia	Gestapo central prison
Weisenbach/Murg	Baden	labor camp
Welden	Bavaria	
Welsheim	Württemberg	camp
Werl	Westphalia	fortress prison
Wernigerode	Saxony	aluminum works
Westerbeck	Oldenburg	transit camp for Jews
Westeregeln	Saxony	Malachit AG
Wetzlar	Hesse-Nassau	housing works
Wewelsburg	Westphalia	
Wiedenbrück	Westphalia	prison
Wien (Vienna)	Austria	prison
Wien-Floridsdorf	Austria	interrogation prison
Wien-Kiln	Austria	disciplinary camp
Wien-Neudorf	Austria	disciplinary camp
Wiener-Neustadt	Austria	camp
Wiener-Neustadt II	Austria	camp
Wilbraudtpuzen	Austria	
Wilhelmshaven	Hanover	disciplinary camp
Wille		
Wilsede		camp
Winterfeld	Saxony	political prisoners
Wismar	Mecklenburg	political prisoners
Wißburg		fortress
Witten/Amen	Westphalia	mines
Witten/Ruhr	Westphalia	mines
Wittenau	Brandenburg	stone quarries
Wittenberg	Saxony	aircraft works
Wittenberge	Brandenburg	political prisoners/Jews
Wittlich	Rhineland	political prisoners
Wittmoor	Hamburg	political prisoners
Witznau		stone quarries
Wlodawa	Poland	political prisoners/Jews

Wöbbelin	Mecklenburg	
Wohlau	Saxony	prison
Woippy-Metz	Alsace	
Wolfach	Baden	prison
Wolfenbüttel	Brunswick	political prisoners
Wolfsberg	Austria	political prisoners
Wollersdorf/Turzdorf	Austria	
Wronchen	Poland	
Wuhlheide	near Berlin	work training camp
Wuppertal	Rhineland	Gestapo prison
Würzburg	Franconia	political prisoners
Wüstegiersdorf	Silesia	camp for Jews
Yastam		
Zabikam	Poland	
Zallarte/Konitz	Poland	
Zams	Austria	political prisoners
Zazel		
Zeiberdorf		
Zeil	Frankfurt	city prison
Zella-Mehlis	Thuringia	weapons factory, labor camp
Zellwolle		
Zement-Ebensee	Austria	
Zgierz	Poland	
Zichenau	Poland	labor camp for Poles
Ziegenberg/Wernigerode	Saxony	political prisoners
Ziegenhain	Hesse	political prisoners
Zielenberg	Silesia	
Zipf		underground construction
Zittau	Saxony	political prisoners
Zlowgow	Poland	
Zörbig	Saxony	lignite mines
Zuchthaus Sonnenburg	Brandenburg	political prisoners
Zweibrücken	Palatinate	political prisoners
Zwickau	Saxony	political prisoners
Zwiebergen	Mecklenburg	underground aircraft works
Zwochau	Saxony	underground V 1 works

Index

About the Compiler and Translator

EUGÈNE ARONEANU, compiler of the accounts, was a Rumanian who was given the task of drawing up the tables of atrocities for the Nuremberg trials. He died prematurely in 1960.

THOMAS WHISSEN, translator of the accounts, is Professor of English, Emeritus, at Wright State University. He is the author of *Isak Dinesen's Aesthetics; A Way with Words; The Devil's Advocates: Decadence in Modern Literature;* and *Classic Cult Fiction: A Guide to Popular Cult Literature* (Greenwood, 1992).

ISBN 0-275-95446-3

HARDCOVER BAR CODE